Take the Measure of the Man
An American Success Story

DANIEL AARON

WITH DAVID A. LONG

FOREWORD BY
RALPH J. ROBERTS

VERITAS PRESS

Take the measure of the man

Take the measure
of the man

AN AMERICAN SUCCESS STORY

DANIEL AARON

WITH DAVID A. LONG

FOREWORD BY RALPH J. ROBERTS

VERITAS PRESS

Veritas Press

Excerpts from The Mills of the Gods *and* A Time to Remember *by Anna Kest Mantinband on pp. 34–35 and 36 are reprinted with permission of the author's estate. Photographs: pp. 90 (top) and 102, Urban Archives, Temple University, Philadelphia, Pa.; pp. 152 and 193 courtesy Comcast Corporation; p. 157, © 1991 by Howard Gordon; all other photographs are from the collection of Daniel Aaron.*

Design by Adrianne Onderdonk Dudden
Composed by Duke & Company

Visit us on the Web at www.danaaron.com and www.takethemeasureoftheman.com

This book may be ordered from Veritas Press, P.O. Box 58070, Philadelphia, Pa. 19102-8070.

To Gerrie

and

To Patricia Ann

Contents

Foreword

Dan Aaron has flair . . . with words, with images. He's always had it. And this book is a testament to that flair. It's hard to put down. You will become engrossed in this fascinating picture of the shaping of a man mentally, physically and spiritually.

Dan's story is a remarkable one—a daring adventure that ranges from the horrors of Nazi Germany to the ultimate and improbable emergence at the pinnacle of one of America's great home-grown industries, cable television. It begins with his escape from Nazi Germany as a young boy, and his arrival in America, where he is soon cast loose from his family by tragic circumstances. He becomes a foster child, acquires an education and a wonderful wife, and then makes a series of career moves, frequently challenged by self-doubt but always showing grit and determination. Ultimately, he becomes a pioneer in the cable industry. I hate to dust off the cliché about a "great American success story," but Dan's is one of the rare tales deserving of that tribute.

Dan is a complex man with the common touch. He is

an intellectual man, and can be passionate about the injustices in the world. Yet at the same time he is a natural-born promoter—he can synthesize a marketing message and convey it in simple and persuasive terms. Dan is like a painter. He pulls you into the picture, subtly shaping your perceptions, and doing it with flair.

Dan combines a compassionate heart with an iron will. He believed in the cable television industry, and gave everything he had to ensure its success. He rose to the chairmanship of the National Cable Television Association, and effectively persuaded our nation's congressional leaders that cable could improve the lives of millions, if only they would provide laws that would encourage its development.

When Dan was afflicted with Parkinson's disease, he fought furiously against its ravages, and he's fighting it still. But his heart reaches out to others who have been victimized by the disease. He has dedicated much of his time in recent years to a foundation to aid Parkinson's sufferers who are less fortunate than he. Dan is a true believer. Anyone, and anything, that tries to slow him down will find out what determination means.

In 1997, when Dan retired from the board of directors of Comcast, the company dedicated a new wing of our cable facility in Sarasota, Florida in his honor. At that time, we presented him a plaque with an inscription reading in part, "[Dan] is a man of superior intelligence, always questioning, and always searching for right answers." Clearly, as he worked to assemble this memoir of a life of challenges and accomplishments, Dan dug deeper than he ever has before for an understanding of himself and what brought him to this place in life. Dan's search is an odyssey for our times, and it is a voyage you will want to share.

Dan has always engendered love and respect among his colleagues at Comcast, and among the many friends he has attracted in Philadelphia and around the nation over the last half-century. It is my privilege to commend my friend Dan's story to you.

RALPH J. ROBERTS
Chairman, Comcast Corporation

Take the measure of the man

When in 1991 Dan Aaron was named Man of the Year by the Movement Disorders Center, a Philadelphia medical institution specializing in the treatment of Parkinson's disease, a crowd of some five hundred friends, business associates and family gathered to honor him.

One of the highlights of the evening was a letter from President George Bush commending Dan, a Parkinson's patient, for his efforts to help others who suffer from Parkinson's. As the President's letter was read wishing Dan and his wife continued success, the crowd rose in a standing ovation.

It was a far different crowd that fifty-five years earlier had looked on while a young Nazi tough in shiny back boots, sporting a swastika armband, followed a young Jewish lad home from school and kicked him full force in the ass with every step he took.

The life of this young man is the tale of this book.

My brother Frank and me, in 1930. Frank was always smiling.

1 *While the crowd looked on*

The Holocaust was not a single event but a series of six million individual tragedies. It decimated my family and spread poisonous roots into families far beyond the estimated six million Jews who were gassed in the chambers of Auschwitz, Buchenwald, Treblinka and other concentration camps.

The Holocaust has maimed generations, and the history of our family recounts the imprint it left on a first-generation survivor. The story of my life is but one example of these catastrophic aftershocks. It is also a tale of survival.

My birthplace is the town of Giessen, Germany, not far from the much larger city, Frankfurt am Main. I was born on January 27, 1926, and four years later my brother, Frank, arrived on the scene. My father, Albert Aaron, was an archetypal German intellectual who ran his family with rigid discipline and unquestioned authority. My mother, Lilli Bamberger Aaron, can best be described by the old German expression, *Kirche, Kuche und Kinder* (church, kitchen and children), the classic put-down of German women. She was a model German Jewish *Hausfrau,* a housewife who took good care of her children, stayed in the kitchen, and knew how to cook and manage a household.

The Aaron family had lived in Germany for more than two hundred years, having arrived in the country in the mid-1700s. My father's parents were farmers and cattle traders whose homestead was located in the *kleine Dorf* (village) of Bobenhausen. After my grandfather's death, my uncle took over the farm, and as youngsters my brother and I would enjoy visiting. My uncle, by then elderly and hard of hearing, dreaded the arrival of his two young, rambunctious nephews who used his hayloft as their gymnasium. But he would put us to work taking cattle from his fields just outside the village limits to his barn in town. I am sure he was amused the day I, at age ten, was pulled all the way home by a lively young calf. I had secured the tether around my wrist and the calf wanted to go back to the barn a lot faster than I did.

Our family home in Giessen was a substantial three-story house with servants, and it had an office on the first floor where my father worked at his lucrative law practice. His practice dealt mainly with the local grain and dairy farmers, drawing up contracts and settling disputes. We considered ourselves to be Germans, living in our native country, practicing Judaism.

By 1933, the son of an obscure Austrian customs official had seized complete control of Germany. The "totalitarian Nazi train" had left the station of civility and begun its headlong plunge into the dark tunnel of bestiality, horror and destruction. Its engineer, not content with his titles of Chancellor and President, declared himself Fuehrer, or leader, of his impoverished nation. So exciting to the German people was this fanatic engineer that few noticed the restrictions placed on women. By 1936, women were forbidden to hold high posts in Germany; female judges were dismissed from office, female doctors and civil servants were unable to find work, and juries were devoid of women. According to chief propagandist Josef Goebbels, "Woman has the task of being beautiful and bringing children into the world."[1] This was just the beginning of restrictions on certain groups of German citizens.

The seeds of German anti-Semitism were sown long before Hitler came to power, and it took only simple encouragement by Goebbels for anti-Semitism to burst into full bloom. What could have been a better vehicle of German solidarity than the tried-and-true doctrine of anti-Semitism? As the "Nazi train" gathered speed on the tracks of hell with its fanatic Fuehrer at the controls, Aryan henchmen would be added as conductors, with names like Himmler, Heydrich, Hess, Eichmann, Goering. It would be Goebbels's duty to head the evil propaganda machine to portray Jews as non-Aryan, subhuman vermin whose total destruction would free Germany of its "tainted blood." With German precision, the "train" would act as the conduit, filling its filthy boxcars with Jewish men, women and children, and transporting them into the network of well-organized extermination camps.

In the early 1930s, my brother and I were confused as to our loyalties. On one hand we were caught up in the excitement that Hitler generated for Germany, but at the same time, as young Jews, we were frightened. A good example of this ambivalence was our reaction to the "magic" of Nazism. The Hitler youth movement organized by Hitler, Goebbels and von Schirach was a "magic bridge" for the

My father, Albert Aaron, was a successful lawyer. With his close-cropped hair, starched shirt and gold watch chain, he looked like a typical German burgher, but he was Jewish. I tried to emulate him; Frank, at right, took a more relaxed attitude.

My mother, Lilli Aaron, was the first to recognize that we were in danger. This photograph was taken during a holiday on the French Riviera that was to be my parents' last vacation.

youth of Germany that stimulated erotic fantasies and visions of youthful abandon. Jewish youngsters were as entranced by the propaganda machine as were their Gentile neighbors.

When Hitler came to our small town, his arrival had all the trappings of a state visit. My family and I joined our Gentile neighbors lining the streets just to get a glimpse of this "magical human being." His visit to Giessen is etched forever in my mind. Hitler was traveling in his open Mercedes amidst a caravan of cars when he insisted the group stop; he had spotted a young blonde child in the crowd. Out of the limousine he bounded as his flunkies clicked their heels and saluted; in his peculiar, awkward stride he advanced to the curb where the child was sitting. As he embraced the child and lifted her high in his arms, Hitler made sure his photographer snapped a picture. The audience went wild; some women fainted while others stamped their feet and screamed, "Heil Hitler, Heil Hitler." I remember being very frightened and was glad when I felt my father's hand in mine, leading me away from the crowd. My father was most uncomfortable too, not knowing when such outbursts of enthusiasm could turn hostile toward Jews.

It was difficult to anticipate how people in our town would react to our presence once they realized that we were Jewish. At one extreme was the *Lumpenproletariat*, a heavily booted, common worker who, sporting a swastika armband, followed me home from school one day and with every step I took, kicked me in the rear. Although there were plenty of adults watching this scene as it unfolded, not one of them stopped him or came to my rescue. He gave up only as I stumbled into our home. I was exhausted, frightened and in pain. I swore that I would some day get even.

When I told my father of this incident and of the steadily

increasing isolation Frank and I felt from our schoolmates, he urged me to join the Zionist Youth Movement. I became an ardent Zionist and wore the uniform that identified me as a member, a white shirt with rolled-up sleeves and blue kerchief. Our white shirtsleeves were always rolled up as a symbol of our readiness to leave for Palestine at any moment. I begged my parents to let me make an *alyiah* to Palestine (a commitment to spend at least a year living and working in what was then called Palestine), but they resisted my pressures out of fear that it would break up our family. My parents could never have imagined then the tragic circumstances of our final separation.

At the other extreme from the *Lumpenproletariat* was the principal of our *gymnasium*. He was a general in the German army and always wore a large swastika on his suit, a fearsome emblem that identified him in my mind as a Nazi and an anti-Semite. When the annual class book was published, it featured a large portrait of Hitler on the first page. Soon afterward, the principal summoned me to his office. You can imagine my anxiety as I walked reluctantly down the hall for our scheduled meeting. But inside the privacy of his study, he told me that if I wanted to tear Hitler's portrait out of the yearbook, I had his permission to do so. He understood; he disapproved of Hitler's attacks on the Jews. To my surprise I realized that he was a friend in disguise.

Our experience told us that there were good Germans, but they were few and far between. One of them was a tailor, an old socialist friend of my father's, who would sneak into our apartment at night to report on the latest events that were taking place in the streets of Germany. Every time he came he had a political joke for us. I remember one of them that was making the rounds: "Two German socialists met on the street and one said to the other, 'Heil Hitler! The dog is dead.' The other socialist cheered." Even the jokes had to be in code; if one dared to openly cheer at talk of Hitler's death, one would have been shot on the spot.

My family was regularly victimized by the German obsession for marching and singing. Uniformed Nazi youths would stop in front of our house and treat us to the following "serenade," *Soldaten, Kameraden* (Soldiers, Comrades). Only recently, while writing these memoirs, I awoke one night from a deep sleep, and the words and tune of this song, which had terrorized me fifty-three years ago, crossed my consciousness.

> *Haengt die Juden;*
> *Stellt die Bunzen an die Wand;*
> *Wenn das Judenblut vom Messer spritzt*
> *Dann gehts noch einmal so gut.*

> (Hang the Jews,
> Up against the wall with the big shot bosses;
> When the Jewish blood spurts from the knife
> We will lead a better life.)

My mother had more understanding of the situation than the rest of the family. She recognized the inherent dangers of the anti-Semitism that was rampant in Germany and the special danger of our position. As she watched Hitler's rise, she realized that Jews were no longer welcome in Germany, but she could not sway my father to leave. My father clung to the belief that his reputation as a successful lawyer and state senator protected him.

My father was a member of the opposition party and a

*My mother's mother,
Sophie Bergmann.*

senator from our local state, Hessen. It was his position as state senator that brought clients to his law office; unfortunately this position also made him a marked man. He had been elected on the Social Democratic ticket, which identified him as an opponent of the Nazi party. It was only a matter of time until Hitler took revenge on any and all that had worked against his party. Worse, we were also Jews.

It took five more years before my father finally succumbed to the realization that he and his family would have to leave his homeland, and only after it became evident that he could no longer practice his chosen profession. The authorities had forbidden him to try cases in the courtroom or attend trials, and it became more and more difficult for him to make a living.

One night, the Nazis abruptly arrested my father and sent him to prison; because he was a member of the opposition party and a Jew, he had become an "undesirable." The Nazis cared nothing for his social standing.

My brother and I watched his arrest from our hiding

place underneath the library table. Amidst the works of the great masters Goethe, Schiller and Kant we looked on in fear and confusion as Father was hustled off to jail. To us, at eleven and eight years, this represented a fearful world gone mad.

What followed was one of the most difficult periods of my life. My family's primary concern was to get my father out of prison long enough for us to escape to the United States. Adding to my anxiety was the regrettable fact that in the late 1930s the United States did not receive German Jewish emigrants with open arms; entrance required sponsorship by an American together with a preferred position on the iniquitous-seeming quota list.

Aunt Bertha Katz, my father's sister who lived in Philadelphia, became our sponsor. She filled out the necessary papers revealing her financial status and assured the government that as refugees, we would not become a burden to the United States. Once that application cleared, an affidavit was issued which Aunt Bertha sent to us. We in turn took this precious document to the consul at the American embassy and applied for a visa.

With all the required paperwork done, we now had to wait for an opening. Not until our number came up on the quota list could we leave the "Fatherland" and emigrate to the United States.

The waiting was excruciating. I remember going to the mailbox every day to see if the entrance papers had arrived. Finally, the necessary papers were there in the box, and our joy and relief was indescribable.

All we needed now was to free Father.

Mother was the one who performed that miracle. She called every professional and nonprofessional my father had known in Giessen, and finally, through sheer perseverance, she succeeded in getting my father released. She also had contrived to purchase open tickets on the steamer from Antwerp to New York and was fully packed and ready to leave at a moment's notice.

For my parents, my father's release was not an occasion of celebration but rather the final impetus for the permanent break with our homeland. For Frank and me it was more exciting than reading adventures written by our favorite writer, Karl May, a famous German writer of teen-age books and ironically, Hitler's own favorite writer.

The timing of Father's release was fortuitous. In the spring of 1937, Hitler had annexed Austria, ostensibly to give his people more living space, a policy he called *Lebensraum*. With the Fuehrer's approval, the Austrian Nazis, now at long last part of the German Nazi machine, were brutalizing the Jews of Austria. *Kristallnacht*, the Night of Broken Glass, would take place the following year: Throughout Germany and Austria, the Nazis shattered storefront windows, burned synagogues, and sent more than 30,000 Jews to concentration camps.

After my father's release from prison, my parents lost no time preparing to leave. Because we were already packed, we completed last-minute details and left almost immediately for the train station. Unfortunately, my mother's mother, Sophie Bergmann, was too feeble to join us, so my parents placed her in a Jewish home in Frankfurt. The prerequisite for entrance into the institution was prepayment for a ten-year period, payable to the German government. What a cruel joke; my Grandmother Bergmann was in her nineties at the time. Mother wrote weekly from her new home in America only to find, within months, that her letters were

En route to America with my father — first class.

returned with the notation, "address unknown." I can only assume that my grandmother perished somewhere in Hitler's deadly network of concentration camps.

On our way to Antwerp, the Nazis came aboard the train to inspect our papers. They were very thorough, inspecting even our prepared sandwiches to make sure we were not taking with us cash or any other forbidden valuables.

Once we reached Antwerp and boarded the ship, the relief of escaping Germany and being away from the terrifying, watchful eyes of the Nazis—coupled with the joy of having his family together again—brought about a change in my father. I saw a side of him that I had never seen before, that of a gentle, loving, devoted head of the family, someone quite different from the person I had viewed as the undisputed head of the household who ruled with an iron hand. The change became clear to me when my father insisted that his children not be forced to sit in the children's dining room, which was located in the third-class section.

In a final splurge before leaving our homeland, my father had purchased first-class tickets for the four of us, and he was adamant that Frank and I should be allowed to dine with him and my mother in first class. The captain of the ship was brought into this argument, but my father stood firm. Frank and I became the only children on board who enjoyed the luxury of first-class dining. The battle Father had waged and won brought comfort to me and strengthened my confidence in his love.

The voyage was an exciting adventure for two boys. With another young passenger we played hide-and-seek, racing around for hours on our luxury liner. The days passed quickly as we three boys investigated all the decks, and before we knew it we were at the entrance to New York Harbor, our gateway to the United States.

2 *The sidewalks of New York*

I was twelve and my brother, Frank, was eight when we arrived in America in 1938. As our ship passed the Statute of Liberty I was impressed with the lady's size as she stood, her flame of freedom held high, greeting "the humble masses yearning to breathe free." But even as I was thrilled by her majesty, I felt worried: I had overheard a passenger express concern about a case of pinkeye discovered on our ship. An outbreak of pinkeye (conjunctivitis) would block our entry into the United States. Fortunately, our ship docked and we disembarked without the dreaded epidemic having materialized.

Our family was spared one of the indignities that most new immigrants endured when arriving in the United States: We did not have to stand for hours in long lines awaiting customs clearance. One of my father's relatives, Tante Jettchen and her daughter, Frances, were there to meet us. My aunt and her family had been farmers in Germany and had arrived just within the past two weeks. Emigration was fresh in their minds, and they knew how to work the system.

With their assistance we were quickly ushered through customs and onto American shores, far from the sound and fury wrought by the Fatherland's "Heil Hitler." At last we were safe—or so we thought—in the "land of the free," a country that believed in tolerance and understanding. Life had to be better here.

These kind, good relatives, whom I warmly remember as simple people of the soil, took us directly from the boat to their apartment in the Bronx, where they housed and fed us for two months. The Bronx in the late 1930s was predominantly a Jewish community where Yiddish was mixed with English and Eastern European languages representing a melting pot of newcomers.

One of my early memories of my new life in America was being given my first American-made children's sleeping garment; this came complete with an attached white scarf to be wrapped around the head as a protection against "bedbugs" or lice. Unfortunately, the scarf didn't work, and after the first night I had to take a head-dunking into a bucket of warm water laced with disinfectant to rid me of the vermin.

If it had not been for the American German Jewish community and the Jewish agencies that they supported, the Jews coming out of Germany during the late 1930s well might have starved. The German Jewish community took these refugees into their homes for weeks at a time until they could be settled in the community. They also acted as sponsors. In the late 1930s the United States government didn't join with the Jewish welfare agencies to give stipends to the Jewish refugees. There was no money for housing, clothing or food, and there were no English or vocational classes to help with assimilation. The government support system that assisted Eastern European refugees coming from Russia in the late 1980s was unavailable to those fleeing the Holocaust.

Since Jewish refugees leaving Nazi Germany were permitted to take only a hundred Reichsmarks per person (at that time $24.00) out of the country, the refugees arrived with little or nothing of monetary value. My parents had spent a great deal of time discussing various ways to conceal their valuables; one that they had discarded as too dangerous was to sew money under the fabric of my mother's dress buttons. They finally decided to secrete the money behind the lens of my father's Leica camera. This hiding place went undetected and Father was able to smuggle 10,000 Reichsmarks out of Germany. When exchanged for American dollars it was not worth very much, not enough to live on for even a year, but my father was convinced that with employment he could supplement the amount. Unfortunately, at that time the United States had just come out of the Great Depression and was heading for a recession, and opportunities for employment were few.

While my brother Frank and I were acclimating ourselves to our new environment, my mother and father were looking around the area in an effort to find a suitable place to settle the family. They picked Kew Gardens in Queens, an upscale community that was a far cry from the poverty of our relatives in the Bronx.

It was in Kew Gardens, where we were to spend our first year, that Frank and I started our Americanization. We hung around the street and learned the skills we needed to participate in street games. As our proficiency increased it was soon forgotten that we were German refugees, and we melded into the group. I was particularly good at "kick the can." (Little did my new friends know that every time I kicked I was imagining that the can was that German thug who had continually kicked me in the ass on my way home from school.) We played chink ball, a form of handball in which the ball had to touch the ground before it touched the wall. Thanks to the other children on the block, we also became proficient in touch football, American style. Half-ball was another of my favorite games; we played with a rubber ball cut in half, using broomsticks for bats. The rules were the same as for baseball, but the size of the playing field was reduced to street size because the bounce had been taken out of the ball.

Another popular street game was called territory, played with an open pocketknife: A rectangle was drawn on the ground and divided into two parts. The object of the game was to stand with both feet inside your own territory and skillfully flip an open knife into the ground of your opponent's territory. Where the blade entered the ground a line was drawn across your enemy's domain, and the larger area became your property. The winner was the one who still had enough territory left to be able to stand in it. What a relief to play with a knife that was not pointed at your throat, as a threat against the "Jew boy."

What a wonderful country this America!

Roller-skating was another of my favorite sports. I loved the feeling of freedom and the wind in my face as I raced down the street with my skates strapped to my shoes. All would go well until I hit a rough spot and a skate would abruptly detach from my shoe, stopping all forward motion except for a stumble and often a fall. The loose skate would dangle uncomfortably around my ankle, held there only by its leather strap. Sitting down on the curb, I would carefully retighten the skate to the sole of my shoe with the skate key that I pulled from my pocket. There was a real trick to getting the skates to stay on my shoes; how tightly I turned the key determined my success or failure. Then I was off again, sailing down the street. My strap-on skates were neat but I coveted the latest model with ball bearings that the other boys had. My father let me know only too quickly that we couldn't afford those.

Once Frank and I were enrolled in school, we were committed to learning English and were required to speak it fluently. In order to hasten this process, our teacher, Miss Gillespie, assigned us to a student who was proficient in Yiddish, as our translator. Assuming that every Jewish newcomer spoke Yiddish, Miss Gillespie felt that this would make learning English easier. What she did not know was that unlike Russian Jews, few German Jews spoke Yiddish.

I was embarrassed to tell my translator that I did not understand a word of his lengthy conversation and that his verbiage was meaningless gibberish. So, instead of understanding his words, I watched his actions and mimicked them. He would raise his hand to ask permission to go to the bathroom; I would raise my hand. He would get up and get in line; I would get up and get in line. I mirrored his every action. I played my part so well that Miss Gillespie was convinced that I was learning English, but in reality I was lost in a sea of Yiddish. The height of this tomfoolery occurred one day when Miss Gillespie became enraged because someone had obviously done something terribly wrong. She demanded that everyone who had participated in the wrongdoing raise his or her right hand. My translator's hand went skyward, and up went mine. Miss Gillespie was particularly disturbed by my participation and singled me out for scolding. To this day I don't know what I admitted to doing. In her singling me out she must have been saying to me, *"Et Tu, Brute"*?

Since then I have learned to love the Yiddish language and its universal appeal to the Jewish community: It expresses a sense of humor, it is earthy, it is emotional, and it reflects the history of the Jewish people.

My father, who was then in his early fifties, was also determined to learn English. He would read the *New York Times* daily and look up in his English-German dictionary every word he could not translate. He felt that this would help him in his pursuit of employment. Unfortunately, there were times when he misunderstood the English meaning completely. For example, when a possible employer would say to him, "Come back and see me sometime," he would take it literally, feeling that he might be getting the job, not realizing it was the employer's way of brushing him off. Colloquial expressions were completely baffling: When Father heard someone use the expression "Yes'um," meaning "Yes madam," he went to the dictionary and looked up "Yes'um" under Y. After not finding it, he finally asked for help.

After we were settled in Kew Gardens, my parents began thinking about my upcoming Bar Mitzvah. I was reaching the age of thirteen, when Jewish boys celebrate their "coming of age" with a Bar Mitzvah ceremony. I had been training in Germany for that sacred ceremony and had memorized my Torah portion.

In every synagogue, one portion of the Torah, or Five Books of Moses, is read each week, beginning with Genesis and continuing in a prescribed orderly sequence throughout the year. Bar Mitzvah students are assigned a reading of that portion of the Torah that falls on the day on which they have their ceremony and which is nearest their thirteenth birthday. The passages are difficult, and take at least a year of preparation for a student to feel comfortable with his Torah portion.

Our synagogue in Kew Gardens served a middle-class Jewish community. In our synagogue there were more Bar Mitzvah boys than dates in the calendar. This meant that often a student would share the spotlight; two families and even three might join together for the Bar Mitzvah celebration.

Two weeks before my scheduled Bar Mitzvah, the rabbi called me into his study to inform me that my special day had been put off by several weeks. The other Bar Mitzvah's family had objected to having their son participate in the Torah reading with a "German refugee" whose family was not of the same social status. As I left the rabbi's study, I was convinced that the whole world was against me. The rabbi's "several weeks" never materialized, and there was no rescheduled date, so I never did have my Bar Mitzvah ceremony.

My brother and I hoped our Americanization process would be intensified by our attendance at a YMCA summer camp located on Staten Island in an area that has since become the site of housing developments. Both Frank and I were fortunate to receive scholarships for the summer. Our welcome at camp was reassuring and held the promise of a joyful summer.

We had been good athletes in Germany, and now, as German refugees turned campers, we thought we would regain our fame as star soccer players and that our country of origin would make little difference. We were like the other boys in camp, just youngsters having fun. But for the first three weeks we didn't feel that way. Our recent experience in Germany had programmed us to feel we were different.

For example, although cleanliness had been an important part of our upbringing, during the first few weeks at camp Frank and I went unwashed by choice. We never went near the showers. We were under the impression that only Jews were circumcised and that if we took showers, everyone would know we were Jewish. The German propaganda machine had been in high gear by the time we left Germany, and we had learned only too well that circumcision meant we were Jewish. Being Jewish meant persecution.

I can remember the day our counselor found out why we were not going to the showers. He persuaded me to join him in the showers and promised that I would be in for a surprise. The surprise was that he, too, was circumcised, even though I knew he was a Gentile. My confusion didn't stop there. As I looked around at the other kids taking showers I noticed that half the campers were circumcised! Could it be that half the kids at this YMCA camp were Jewish?

My counselor and I became friends and for the next weeks I was the best-scrubbed and cleanest kid in camp.

What a strange country this America!

Once we shed our fear of being thought different, Frank and I began enjoying all the camp activities and winning many of the athletic trophies that were awarded at the end of the season, especially in swimming. We were getting used to the American institutions, making friends, and generally becoming accustomed to American life—or at least the American life as it was carried on at camp. I still remember the songs we sang: *"Frère Jacques,"* "Row, Row, Row Your Boat," and "Short'nin' Bread" ("Mammy's little babies love short'nin', short'nin', Mammy's little babies love short'nin' bread"), a

Lilli and Albert Aaron.

song we sang with gusto, totally unaware of its insensitive racist message. Our experiences that first year at camp were idyllic, and we looked forward to another carefree summer the following year. Little did we know what lay ahead.

In the summer of 1939, my mother's health deteriorated, and after Frank and I had left for our second season at camp, she developed pneumonia. One night my brother and I were awakened at camp in the middle of the night to take a phone call; half-asleep, the only word that I could identify over the phone was "suicide." This was my mother's answer to the pressures of living as an immigrant in the United States: The stress of her illness, her mother's disappearance, the language she did not understand, and the loss of her former economic status were beyond her ability to cope.

My brother and I were rushed home to a cemetery where a few friends had gathered to bury our mother, another victim of the Holocaust.

I remember how shocked I was at how Father looked; he had lost a great deal of weight and was literally down at his heels. He had been looking for work but to no avail. No thanks to the American Bar Association, he was forbidden to practice law, and the jobs available, such as elevator operator or night watchman, were filled by those with less education but greater strength.

I recall little of my mother's funeral except that my father, my brother and I held hands. And I remember suppressing my tears in order not to further upset Father.

After the funeral, we sought counsel among the few relatives that we had, and some decisions were made that were not to become known to us children until later. In the meantime we were rushed back to finish our camp season. Camp was the only support we could hold on to, and we tried to reestablish our life as good campers. But children can be cruel, and two youngsters made us very uncomfortable by teasing us about our situation.

Now a new fear entered my life: At the funeral my father's appearance had distressed me greatly, and I sensed Father's oncoming nervous breakdown. I remember going to bed each night and saying my Hebrew prayers—

Shema Yisraeil Adonai Eloheinu, Adonai Echad
(Hear oh Israel, the Lord our God, the Lord is One)

—and ending by pledging loyalty to God if only God would help my father. I was not sure there was a God, but just in case there was, I wanted His help. But my prayers were unanswered.

Just three weeks after my mother's death, another night

at camp was interrupted by another call—a message that my father had taken his own life. The Holocaust had again taken its toll.

The camp director drove Frank and me to New York, racing to get to the funeral in time. I was physically numb and mentally drained, confused and incoherent. I drew my brother closer to me. We were two boys learning to grapple with the aftershocks of a cataclysm.

At the cemetery we walked hand in hand to the graveside where gravediggers were finishing the process of digging the grave. In a flash I saw us both jumping into the grave with our father. But this scene was immediately exorcised by a conscious effort to force myself to concentrate positively about a coming event, the next day's championship soccer game at camp in which I was expected to star. It may have been a thirteen-year-old's insight into what eventually became cognitive therapy.

An observer at my father's funeral would have seen two boys clutching one another as they were joined at the graveside by a few mourners and by the same ten adult males who had attended my mother's funeral. These men were professional mourners and formed the minyan. To qualify for a minyan a Jewish male must be thirteen years old and must have celebrated his Bar Mitzvah. Unfortunately, although I was thirteen, I could not qualify for the minyan because I had been denied my Bar Mitzvah ceremony. The *davening* mourners said the mourner's kaddish, ending with the traditional Hebrew blessing. The following is an English adaptation from the Aramaic:

May the Source of peace send peace to all who mourn,
And comfort to all who are bereaved. Amen.

When the service was completed, an observer would have been puzzled to see the younger of the two boys pause at the next grave, where he knelt and cried. A mound of dirt identified it as a recently dug grave; this was the grave of their mother. As the funeral ended, and the mourners dispersed, the two boys turned around for a last look at the graves of their parents.

When I asked how our parents committed suicide, I was told that this was a subject not to be discussed among children. By the time I built up the courage to again ask that question many years later, all the relatives who knew of that event were deceased.

I never did find out how my parents died. Perhaps I didn't really want to know.

After the funeral, my brother and I were driven back to our apartment in Kew Gardens. I was shocked. It was as though a neutron bomb had exploded and the explosion had preserved all the physical trappings but had vaporized the beloved residents.

For the first few months after our parents' deaths, I found myself anesthetized to all that went on around me. My main concern was to make sure that my little brother and I survived. So numbed were my feelings that I couldn't even react to the ugly remarks from some of the kids at camp who taunted us by saying, "Your parents committed suicide."

But the anesthesia soon wore off, and getting to sleep at night became a problem. Thoughts swirled through my head. The questions were endless: What brought them to suicide? How could they leave two young boys in a strange land to fend for themselves? How could they be so selfish? Were we that bad? Didn't they love us? Why did this happen to us?

These tragic events left me with a permanent emotional scar. I had to learn to control my emotions, and it became difficult for me to let others know how I felt.

3 *The slippery welcome mat*

It was obvious to all that two boys, ages thirteen and nine, couldn't go back to their empty apartment in Kew Gardens, and it was Aunt Bertha Katz and her family who offered help.

Aunt Bertha lived in a rowhouse at the intersection of Broad and Olney in Philadelphia with her husband, Adolph, who ran a successful travel business. Living nearby was Aunt Bertha's married daughter, Frances, and her son-in-law, Mark Baum, a furniture buyer at Stern's department store.

Our stay of several weeks was difficult. At the age of sixty, this poor woman, my aunt and sponsor, had to provide a domicile not only for her family but also for two traumatized and active boys. I can remember only too well the ruckus we caused when we broke the beak off her prized porcelain bird. Frank and I were just too much for Aunt Bertha to handle, and within the month we were packed off to the Association for Jewish Children, the Philadelphia agency that took care of destitute orphans. However, for the duration of our stay as wards of AJC, Aunt Bertha's daughter, Frances Baum, periodically took us to lunch at our favorite restaurant, Horn and Hardart's automat in the Germantown section of Philadelphia.

Eating at the automat was an adventure. Entrance into the restaurant disclosed units of shiny chrome-edged windows surrounded by gleaming white enamel. On closer inspection the windows revealed short-order dishes, plates of salad, sandwiches, oranges and apples, and pies of all kinds. The windows were made of milk glass with beveled edges, and they presented a wondrous sight, beckoning us forward. In order to obtain the treasured contents secured behind the windows, we placed nickels, dimes and quarters into the slot provided. One of the thrills of being at the automat was hearing the *click, click, click* as the coins hit the bottom of the money receptor. Then, with a turn of the white enameled handle, the window would magically spring open, allowing access to the food inside.

Cousin Frances would give us the required change, and off Frank and I would go for our treats. We always made the same selection: baked beans and two slices of whipped cream pie. When we brought our food to the table, our cousin would invariably send us back to return one of the desserts and instead choose a vegetable. After lunch at the automat, we'd take in the local Saturday afternoon movie at the Bandbox theater. It was the highlight of our week.

In better times Frank and I would have been placed in the Foster Home for Hebrew Orphans, a large stone institution located on Church Lane in Germantown. FHHO had been serving the Jewish community for more than fifty years, housing as many as two hundred orphans at a time. Its president was Leo Heimerdinger, who was part owner of the Pioneer Belt and Suspender Company. The agency's reputation was impeccable. (Little did I realize then that the future owner of the Pioneer Belt and Suspender Company, Ralph Roberts, would later play such a prominent role in my future.) Unfortunately, with the influx of so many Jewish refugees from Germany and Eastern Europe, the FHHO was fully occupied. An alternative was the foster home program sponsored by the Association for Jewish Children. It was into this setting that my brother and I were placed.

Poor Jewish families owned many of the foster homes, and their primary motivation was not always the welfare of their foster children; often, it was to augment their incomes. In Jules Doneson's history of Jewish foster home care in Philadelphia, *Deeds of Love,* he writes, "More than a few of the 'boarding out' placements were unsuccessful. Families were more interested in receiving the $25 to $30 a month than in welcoming the new arrival."[2] In due course my brother and I crossed the thresholds of no fewer than six separate homes, and most of our foster home experiences were disasters. I had thought we were placed in these foster homes to help us become Americans. If that was the aim, most of them did so very poorly.

To add to our misery, our "social workers" were ill equipped for the task of visiting their clients. Very few at that time had an M.S.W. (Master of Social Work), the degree needed for employment in the field today. Worse, because of a heavy caseload, our caseworker visited us only once a month, hardly enough time to understand what problems we children might be having adjusting to our foster home.

At our monthly meeting with the social worker, we received an allowance of fifty cents. This was accompanied by a document which we had to sign, indicating that any money earned beyond the fifty cents would be turned over to the agency.

Our relationship with the social worker became one of a detective and possible thieves. For example, I had a job delivering Sunday breakfasts of lox and bagels to Jewish homes in the area. I purchased my supplies from a local distributor, sorted them in bags and delivered them to my customers. The area was large enough for me to need a bicycle, for which I paid a rental fee. My customers were pleased with my service and many times would tip me. I felt that this money should belong to me even though the rules of the agency were unequivocal. It became a constant battle between my social worker and me.

One of the things I looked forward to during this period was the annual suit distribution by the Association for Jewish Children. Once a year, all the boys living in foster homes were taken to Goldsmith's Manufacturing Company for what was described as their "new suit fitting." Once inside the factory, we would stand in line with great anticipation, waiting to be fitted for our new suits. I can still remember that pungent factory smell of freshly cut cloth. To me that pleasant smell meant one new suit. As we progressed to the front of the line, one of the factory workers would request our age, and after a quick look at our physique, determine what size suit we would need. At the head of the line, we were given a choice: Did we want a brown herringbone or blue serge suit? That decision made, we were handed the suit wrapped neatly in kraft paper. We were thrilled. As to the fit, that was another story; I never did see a suit that actually fit anyone. Either the pants were too long, the shoulders too wide or the sleeves too short. That is where I learned the song, "Sammy, You Made the Pants Too Long." But it really didn't matter. We had a new suit. Foster home girls weren't left out;

they went to another factory where they were "fitted" with dresses.

After several temporary placements in foster homes, according to my summary case card from AJC, Frank and I were scheduled in March of 1940 to be placed in a "permanent home."

My brother and I were about to be rescued by the Mantinband clan of Williamsport, Pennsylvania: Rabbi Charles Mantinband, who liked to be called Uncle Charlie; his wife, whom we would call Aunt Anna; and their two children, Carol and Billy. The rabbi said, as he did whenever he was introduced, "Think of me as the man on the tin band."

Rabbi Mantinband was a rotund figure of a man whose weak eyesight required him to wear thick glasses. He was a man of great intellect and immense warmth who related well to people, and he had strict morals that guided him through life. As rabbi, he was the spiritual leader of the Reform Temple Beth Ha-Shalom, and he was determined to help Frank and me heal the wounds we had suffered since our arrival in the United States. Uncle Charlie and Aunt Anna, the *Rebbitzen* (rabbi's wife), were totally committed to turning us into Americans and, if at all possible, into joyous Americans. Magically, they succeeded.

It was no accident that we became members of the Mantinband family. Carol Mantinband was headed for college in the fall of 1939, and Billy, age fourteen, was to be home alone. When the Association for Jewish Children put out a call for more foster parents, the Mantinbands answered with the stipulation that the child be a boy close to Billy's age. Their application was accepted and their home was promptly investigated. But a year passed before they were

*Our new family—from left, Rabbi Charles Mantinband, the "Man
on the Tin Band"; my brother, Frank; Carol Mantinband; Anna
Mantinband; Billy Mantinband; and me.*

informed that there were two brothers, ages fourteen and
ten, that the agency did not wish to separate: Would they
consider taking both? The Mantinbands agreed, and Frank
and I entered the Mantinbands' home in March of 1940.

Uncle Charlie showed us what he was about the day we
arrived. To introduce us to our new Williamsport home, we
were accompanied by a social worker from the Association
of Jewish Children. During the course of conversation between our social worker and our new foster parents, "Miss
Agency" explained that I had a habit of reading the *New
York Times* on a regular basis. I had started buying the *Times*
a year earlier, using part of my allowance to do so, and I
hardly missed a day. My social worker let Uncle Charlie
know that she considered it too expensive a habit and she,
on occasion, had ordered that I return the paper to the news-

stand. For Uncle Charlie this was an opportunity to take over. I can still hear him say, "My dear lady, in Philadelphia you are in charge. In Williamsport, I am in charge. This boy can read the *New York Times* if he chooses to do so." That shut up "Miss Agency" pronto. Wouldn't Mr. Ochs, publisher of the *New York Times*, have been pleased?

For a description of our first day in Williamsport, I quote from Aunt Anna's essay, *The Mills of the Gods:*

Two tired, fearful and bewildered boys followed a middle-aged woman down the steps of the Pennsylvania train station in Williamsport. The younger one, Frank, age 10, a blond blue-eyed youngster wearing a sweater buttoned over a white shirt atop long pants, seemed more curious than frightened. He jumped down the steps quickly, as if eager to leave the constraints of a long train ride. His brother, Dan, 14, dark-haired and taller, showed strain, and looked at first glance as if he were trying to keep a stiff upper lip against the uncertainties of a new life they were about to enter.

Arriving home, we introduced the boys to our spacious apartment with a large back yard for outdoor play space. A quick shower and change out of travel clothes was followed by a good hot supper. Seated around the table, as the food was served and the blessing said, Charles asked,

"Where did you have lunch, boys? On the train?" A nod.

"What did you have?"

"Two sandwiches and an apple," said Frank quickly.

"No ice cream?" Head-shaking.

"We'll have to make up for that. Do you like ice cream?" A vigorous nod was the reply.

After supper Charles suggested we take our three boys to see *Pinocchio,* playing that evening at the local movie.

The night air was cool and refreshing when the movie

ended; we walked the mile home with a million stars lighting the way. Frank and Dan were transformed from the tensions of their arrival a few hours earlier, and, with Billy were all but dancing in the road while they tried to recapture some of the songs in the film. A dish of ice cream out of the refrigerator ended the day.[3]

Our new home was quite a different world from the flat streets of Queens. Williamsport is in the very heart of Pennsylvania, situated on the west branch of the Susquehanna River, and nestled comfortably among the Appalachian Mountains. Its topography gives it a natural beauty. From any spot in town one can see the densely wooded mountains. In these mountains Uncle Charlie and local ministers from all faiths would take weekly hikes and discuss interdenominational projects.

In the early 1900s lumber was king in Williamsport, and wealthy lumber barons built magnificent brick and stone mansions on Fourth Street on the west side of town. It was into this still-affluent community that Frank and I were placed. The rabbi's home was large enough to have two families living under one roof. Its rooms were spacious, with high ceilings and wide windows overlooking the tree-lined street. Uncle Charlie housed his family on the second and third floors while the local high school biology teacher lived on the first floor. The teacher was a birdwatching enthusiast who taught us the difference between a cardinal and a chickadee.

Most of our activities were within walking or biking distance, and Frank and I were given bikes by some kind soul in the community. The center of town was a brisk ten-minute walk, and the synagogue was conveniently closer. I would spend many a day in town looking at a men's department store, "The Hub," daydreaming about the clothes I would love to own.

The new high school, with its separate gymnasium, had been built in 1936 of yellow brick, and was just around the corner from our house. When I left Germany two years earlier I had been a ninth grader but had studied English for only half a year, and my Yiddish tutor in Queens had not been much help, despite his best efforts. When I entered Williamsport High, my English was so limited that I was enrolled as a second grader. But with the help of an understanding teacher I soon became a sophomore.

Like others whose native tongue was German, I had great difficulty with the diphthong "th." It requires that one's tongue be held between the teeth and quickly withdrawn to get the elusive "th" sound. In the German language there is no "th" sound. Because of this, a native German when faced with the word "the" will pronounce it as "se."

My Williamsport high school teacher, Mrs. Wendell, was convinced, and rightfully so, that if I kept my German accent I would not be able to succeed in her native land. She was resolved to do something about it and her cure was simple: Every time the class was assigned a composition, I was called in front to read mine. The utterance of the word "the" as "se" would prompt her to stop my reading until I pronounced "the" the American way. It was enough to make me quit school or lose my accent; fortunately, I chose the latter.

From reading the *Rebbitzen's* memoirs, *A Time to Remember*, it seems as if my brother and I quickly become enmeshed in the fabric of the Mantinband family. Shortly after our arrival, Frank and I were playing with Billy in the back yard when a visitor asked Aunt Anna, "Which is yours?"

"I'll have to think," she replied; "they get equally scolded."[4]

My personal remembrance is one of ambivalence. For

me, an orphaned German refugee, becoming part of the Mantinband family filled part of the vacuum of family identity created by my losses. On the other hand, I felt like an outsider who, because of circumstances, was being pushed and pulled in all directions to accept this unknown quantity called the Mantinband family. This in no way negates the love the Mantinbands gave. They could not have been more sympathetic or more embracing, and they truly understood the difficulties my brother and I had been through.

Billy was most threatened by these new relationships. The sole attention he had been getting from his parents would have to be shared now with two new "brothers." To his credit, he tried to make us feel welcome, and Carol became the big sister we never had. We became close and have kept in touch with each other throughout the years.

Frank and I stuck together like glue. In a sense, I became his father figure, and he became an integral part of my support system. I reveled in Frank's accomplishments as a good-looking "jock," and he in mine as an "intellectual." The Mantinbands had kindly given us our own room, and though our quarters had two beds, we used only one. Our nighttime ritual was always the same: Before we retired for the night, we gave each other a big hug and then crawled into bed together.

In order to augment my allowance I began caddying at the local Jewish country club. The game of golf seemed to bring out the worst in people; a golfer who was having a poor day could always blame his caddy for giving him the wrong club. But I soon mellowed in my attitude toward the golfers. Every week one afternoon was set aside as "caddy's day," and as I took advantage of the free golf days I learned only too quickly how frustrating the game of golf can be.

I also made extra money by setting pins in the local bowling alley. This dangerous occupation tested my patience and my ability to escape a twenty-five-pound bowling ball rolling down the alley at fifty miles an hour, often hurled not only with the intent to make a score but also to hit the pinsetter. In those days there was no such contraption as an automatic pin-setting machine. To set the heavy pins in place one needed a skilled, agile lad who could spot the pins on their predetermined site and who could straddle the alley while the bowler made his shot. The trick was to get high enough to escape the thundering ball and the flying pins. The routine was simple: Set up and straddle the lane, set up and straddle.

I don't remember what I did with my extra earnings, but I certainly didn't have enough to buy those clothes I coveted. I am sure I used some of it for good purposes which included giving a fair share to the weekly Sunday school collection for the poor. Contributions also found their way into the blue *tzedakah* box (charity box) at home. This money was used to plant trees in a land that would within the decade become the State of Israel.

Years later, when I established my own family, I realized that many of my values were based on principles that I had learned from Uncle Charlie. This was particularly true of my attitude toward money. For me, money had been the only way to deal with the envy I held towards others more fortunate than I. In my sense of insecurity, money seemed to make the difference. Uncle Charlie enabled me to understand that money alone did not produce happiness.

Everyone knew Uncle Charlie's salary because the financial report of the synagogue was open knowledge. His salary was adequate but certainly not generous. Yet in spite of their limited income, Uncle Charlie and Aunt Anna managed to become involved in every social cause and activity in Williamsport. The Jewish High Holy Days were occasions for reflection and remembrance and not a venue to display fur coats, jewelry and other current fashions. These, to Uncle Charlie and Aunt Anna, required expenditures that should have been turned into donations to Jewish causes.

Uncle Charlie and Aunt Anna set an example of how to live life, letting humor soften their most difficult experiences, and their enjoyment of life was infectious. They showed us how to stick to one's principles and not to be intimidated by wealth or power. Uncle Charlie was not impressed by the country club set and their ostentation. His only surrender to the required rabbinical dress code, that of a suit and tie, was a fresh shirt every day. His wife would inspect him before he left the house and remind him that blue and green didn't match.

Aunt Anna defined her role as a true partner to her husband and his interests. She admired him, she loved him, and she guarded him. At the same time she could expand that love and guidance to two orphaned boys. Aunt Anna also led a monthly book review that was the intellectual highlight of the community, she was an amateur actress, and she played her role as *Rebbitzen* to perfection.

Aunt Anna's Friday night Sabbath services at home were happy occasions. A special tablecloth, challah, sweet wine and candles always blessed her Sabbath dinner table. Never content to entertain just the family, she would invite friends from the community or any visiting dignitaries to join us. On one such occasion the renowned Rabbi Stephen S. Wise, an ardent Zionist and head of the Free Synagogue in New York City, visited us. His features were stern and intimidating, and we children were awed and frightened by his presence. Aunt Anna, sensing our discomfort, began talking about her recent trip to Broadway where she had seen *The Man Who Came to Dinner.* Laughter soon cleared the strained atmosphere.

Friday service attendance at the temple was compulsory. In synagogue I would join in the formal prayers and I listened closely to Uncle Charlie's sermon. But I never again prayed to the God who tested his flock as he had tested my brother and me.

In Williamsport I became active in the local chapter of the YMCA, where, much to Uncle Charlie's surprise, I was elected president of the youth club. I can still see the consternation on the face of the very conservative adult advisor as he tried to deal with the German Jewish refugee who had been elected president of the Williamsport Young Men's Christian Association.

It is interesting to note how the YMCA played a significant role in my life, first when I was a camper in New York during the most tragic period of my life, and again when I was president of the Williamsport chapter. These were landmarks in my development, and my success demonstrated the broad tolerance of this Christian institution devoted to integrating members of various faiths.

Another organization, the Elks Lodge of Williamsport, had an annual essay contest on the subject of "What It Means to Be an American." Uncle Charlie thought this would be a great way for me to become more acclimated to America, and, equally important, for the community to know that there was a young German refugee in their ranks. I felt otherwise, but to appease Uncle Charlie I said I would try. I frankly didn't think there was a chance in hell that I could compete against a class of American youngsters in a language that was native to them while foreign to me.

Uncle Charlie proved to be right: Not only could I write the article, but my composition was picked as a winner and my picture and essay appeared in the *Williamsport Sun*. A reporter for the *Sun* interviewed me and quoted me as saying, "I admire the sportsmanship in the elections in this country. After the fighting is over, the candidates join forces for national defense. 'Over there,' if there is an election, the loser usually gets shot."

The award came with a $15 savings bond. I was ecstatic! I remember that day clearly. After learning that I had won the contest I ran all the way home, wound up my 78 RPM record player and, at full blast, played my favorite song, sung by that great African-American actor and singer, Paul Robeson: It was called "Ballad for Americans."

That so much attention would be given to a Jewish kid from Germany bothered one of the Christian clergy. He wrote a letter to the newspaper complaining that in giving the Pledge of Allegiance in school, a ritual that preceded the daily prayer, I had done so with my palm facing down instead of facing up. In the early 1940s one pledged allegiance to the flag with an outstretched arm and an upward palm. Based on information from one of my classmates, the reverend alleged that I was really giving the Nazi salute.

Once again in my young life I was called to the principal's office. The walk down the hall to his office proved just as upsetting as it had in Germany. My principal wanted to know what the commotion was all about. I told him that I knew the difference between palm up and palm down: One was the Pledge of Allegiance to the flag, the other the Nazi greeting. He believed me, and the whole ugly incident was dropped. (Later, the positioning of the pledge was changed by government order; instead of extending the hand and arm, one placed the hand over one's heart, never again to be taken for a Nazi salute.)

But Uncle Charlie did not let the matter rest. He decided we should make the rounds of the local service clubs where I would recite my article. Subsequently I visited members of the Lions Club, the American Legion and the Moose Lodge. These community leaders were delighted with my article and were pleased that a kid from Germany would get up in front of a group and recite his article about being an American.

I enjoyed after-school activities and became a member of the tennis and gym teams. The prerequisite for joining the gym team required skills in acrobatics, tumbling, and balance. I became particularly proficient on the rings, and was able to perform an "iron cross" and at times a dismount or "flyaway." Debating was another activity. Williamsport in those days was a stronghold of the Republican Party, and the party faithful would insist on pronouncing President Roosevelt's name as "Roooosevelt" in an uncomplimentary way. Republicanism was so deeply seated in the community that when the principal of our high school asked for volunteers to represent the Democratic side in a local debate, he was unable to find a single volunteer. In desperation he called me. So I represented the Democrats of Williamsport and soon became known as "Mr. Democrat." It was hard to believe that in all of Williamsport, my principal couldn't find a Democrat other than an alien.

During high school I also became an avid football fan, but the cost of attending out-of-town games was beyond my limited means. When I found out that our school band-leader was having trouble filling the post of a tuba player,

I volunteered. I knew that the band played during half time at all football games, and I also knew that by volunteering I would be able to attend all the football games at no cost. So I accepted the bandleader's offer to take the required weekly lessons. There are few instruments brasher than the tuba. The performer rarely plays a tune and the instrument weighs a ton. My family found my practicing increasingly annoying, but we finally reached an agreement; I would practice my tuba in the small park not far from home. I never did find out what the neighbors thought of the strange *oompapas* coming from their park! Uncle Charlie's comment was very reassuring; he said that it was no less difficult getting an audience for his sermons than it was finding an audience for my tuba playing.

Frank and I remained in Williamsport with the Mantinbands until the fall of 1941, when our lives were disturbed by drastic change.

As it became evident that the United States could not avoid involvement in the war that had already engulfed Europe, the Jewish Welfare Board called Uncle Charlie into service. He had been a United Service Organization worker in World War I, and when the organization asked him to take charge of the U.S.O. at the Aberdeen Proving Grounds in Maryland, he accepted.

The transition was abrupt, and my brother and I were once again in turmoil, without roots, facing another unknown. Leaving the Mantinbands and Williamsport was a very sad day. The Mantinbands had showed us how beautiful life could be in America. I had acquired a circle of good friends and was beginning to feel that Williamsport was home. All of this came to a screeching halt.

Uncle Charlie and Aunt Anna sent this photograph commemorating their golden wedding anniversary in 1968.

An attempt was made to find a family in Williamsport who would take in Frank and me so that we might finish high school there. Unfortunately, no one volunteered.

I must confess that I was embittered by the sudden breakup of what had become our home. Even though I realized that many homes were disrupted by the war, I felt that having opened their home to us, the Mantinbands had assumed a responsibility that they shed too easily. Aunt Anna must have shared similar feelings, because later she mentioned her regrets over the way we parted. Nevertheless, Frank and I maintained a relationship with the Mantinbands for the rest of their lives. They encouraged my brother Frank to attend college, and provided room and board for him while he was in school at the University of Alabama, and they made themselves available whenever we needed help or advice.

4 *There is no place called home*

Frank and I were returned to Philadelphia by the Association of Jewish Children and placed temporarily in a home in West Philadelphia. During the next two months we would pack and unpack our meager belongings three times. It was October 1941, less than two months before the Japanese attack on Pearl Harbor. That winter, a foster home was located with Mrs. Lena Myers on Catherine Street in West Philadelphia, where Frank and I would spend the next two years.

Lena Myers was the salt of the earth. Although financially poor, she was rich with the wealth of love, advice and understanding that she gave to her foster children. She exemplified the AJC's foster home program at its best. She had great pride in keeping her home spotless and her foster children well groomed. Every night she would wash our clothes for the following day. She could ill afford a washer with a wringer; a dryer was out of the question. Instead she used a scrubbing board, wrung the laundry by hand, and, on sunny days, hung the wash on the line to dry. Midnight was her time to iron our shirts for the next day's use.

Friday afternoons, Lena Myers would be on her knees scrubbing and waxing the floors in preparation for the Sabbath. After the floor was spick-and-span, the clean surface would be covered with newspapers that had been collected all week for that purpose. Saturday evening at sundown the papers would come up and the sparkling floors would sanctify our home, as in every Jewish home in the area. Little did Moses Annenberg know that little old ladies with scrub brushes boosted the circulation of his newspaper, the *Inquirer.*

One of my jobs for Mrs. Myers was to stoke the basement coal furnace every night. The idea was to keep the furnace going throughout the night, using as little fuel as possible; coal was an expensive commodity. Banking the coal with just the right amount of fuel took time and practice, but I can report there were few cold nights due to an unfired furnace.

Mornings were the reverse. On cold mornings the alarm would go off at six; I would jump out of bed, shivering, and run down to the cellar to breathe fresh life into the banked embers. Shoveling coal from the bin like an automaton, I would stoke the furnace as fast as I could, then charge back upstairs and dive under the covers to catch another hour's sleep. By the time the second alarm sounded at seven, the house would be warm and toasty. Oh, how I hated that work detail! It was the coal furnace that taught me a whole new vocabulary of American curse words.

Twice a week, Frank and I would collect the ashes, shoveling them through the basement's small window into large metal containers. We would then lug the heavy containers to the curb so the Department of Sanitation could dispose of the spent fuel.

Everyone on the block knew when coal was being delivered. The large dump truck, sitting with its rear wheels on the sidewalk, had a black metal chute extending from the back of the truck through the basement window into the coal bin. The grating sound of the coal rattling down the coal chute into the cellar bin had a pitch and tone of its own and announced to the neighborhood that the coal bills were paid up. To this day I can still hear that unique noise.

"Foster Mother Myers" had little formal schooling of her own, but she worshipped education as a way out of poverty. Although she probably could not understand them, she insisted on seeing all marks that Frank and I received from school. Should we fall below an A or the mark of 90, she would scold us. She taught us that poverty was just another obstacle to overcome. Lena Myers lived in a different stratum of society than did the Mantinbands, and the contrast reminded me that the quality of family life does not depend on financial resources alone. However, my lack of finances represented an important limitation.

Central High School in Philadelphia was the most prestigious public school in the city. An all-male school, it boasted of high academic scholarship and was an excellent preparatory institution for college. It was the school of choice for all the boys who were scholastically above average, a magnet school serving the entire Philadelphia area. Central was where I wanted to go. Unfortunately, the public transportation costs of getting to and from Central were beyond my means. Simply put, I didn't have the fifteen-cent carfare. Sweet woman that she was, Lena Myers offered the remainder of her savings account to pay for my public transportation. I would not hear of it, and I entered West Philadelphia High School, or "West Philly High." (It is one of the wonders of America that at the end of the century, one of my grandsons would graduate from Central High School as captain of its vaunted tennis team.)

My school experience in Williamsport had been almost idyllic. The teachers there had taken a special interest in my education and had challenged me to expand my intellectual horizons. West Philly High was a different story. I was lost amidst a much larger student body; I felt that I intruded upon relationships that had been developed among students for years; I was an outsider. To be thrust into the vast educational mill of West Philadelphia High School was traumatic, and my reaction was one of great anger. I had lost not only my stable home and all my friends in Williamsport, but I was being forced to attend a school that was not of my choosing. I acted out my ire and frustration in my first term at West Philly by intentionally flunking every course I took.

It was my summer work at a camp for poor Jewish boys, the S.G.F. Vacation Camp, that gave me a new lease on life.

The S.G.F. Vacation Camp, located on the property of the Lubin Motion Picture Company, had been founded in 1921 by Samuel G. Friedman, Edward L. Espen, and Mrs. Frank Pfaelzer. Samuel G. Friedman, an insurance broker and scoutmaster of Boy Scout Troop 95, decided to extend the troop's summer activities by providing camping experience. After a few years, a property of 120 acres was secured for the camp near Collegeville, Pa. Later, the scope of S.G.F. was enlarged from that of serving Scout Troop 95 to providing camping experience for disadvantaged boys. Campers and funds were provided by several organizations, and when the Federation of Jewish Agencies accepted S.G.F. into the Federation in 1944, this act assured the camp a steady stream of financial support and enabled it to expand from 72 campers to 131.[5]

During the summer of 1942, I desperately needed a job

and answered an ad for camp counselors that was listed in the *Jewish Exponent* (the weekly journal of local, national and international Jewish news published by the Philadelphia Federation of Jewish Agencies). I had already been turned down by a local private camp and was pleased when I received word that S.G.F. could use my services for the summer.

What was to be one summer's work turned into six, resulting in enduring relationships with campers and staff who became lifelong friends. S.G.F. became the single institution to which I had the closest loyalty; it was my fraternity, my alumni association. Interestingly, most of my new friends were achievers who became leaders of their professions and their communities. Beginning as a counselor, I would climb the ladder of responsibility to head counselor, director, board member and ultimately, president of the board at twenty-six, the youngest president of any agency in the Federation of Jewish Agencies.

Marty Foreman became my closest friend. Later, Marty's wife, Elaine, and my wife, Gerrie, joined that friendship. Marty was a handsome, winning young man with street charm and an athletic build, although he was slightly bow-legged. We were the same age. He was my social role model, and I his intellectual mentor. At campfires he convulsed thousands of delighted campers with his rendering of the "Baloney Song." The final refrain will be familiar to many—

I dreamt you wasn't coming back
So I ate the baloney.

S.G.F. campers called Marty Uncle Zeke, and they adored him; as an underprivileged kid, he was one of them. Marty

Marty Foreman was my main supporter at Camp S.G.F. This snapshot was taken during my last summer there, in 1947.

No money, no contacts, no prospects — no problem! At Camp S.G.F., for the first time in my life I was a big shot.

was brought up on Philadelphia's "lower East Side" in South Philly, in the same kind of rowhouse with which I was familiar. Marty never forgot his roots. He was the best athlete on the block but opted for a Ph.D. in sociology. When he died at the age of fifty, he had been in charge of the Food for Peace Program for the State Department, and it was generally regarded that he would have been nominated for a Nobel Peace Prize for his outstanding work in fighting hunger throughout the world. Marty was a pied piper, a leader emulated by youngsters and peers alike. He enriched my small world by his embrace, as he would later embrace the globe.

Another lifelong camp friend is Val Udell, a bachelor who was "married" to camp and beloved and admired by campers and adults alike. Val studied all the campers' names to make them feel welcome. I marveled at the way he could walk around camp greeting each boy by his first name. Remembering names has always been a problem to me, and Val's skill was even more amazing considering a new crop of campers arrived every two weeks. Val revealed the raptures of nature to city boys and taught them to distinguish one bird from another and to appreciate the natural world around them. Val mesmerized campers. In later years Val would spend many an evening with my wife and me, discussing politics and our plans for S.G.F.

That first summer at S.G.F., when I was sixteen, I was hired as a counselor to boys who were not much younger than I. It was a joy to be part of the camp scene again, and I thoroughly enjoyed myself. Because S.G.F. was a camp for underprivileged boys, many of whom came from broken homes or were orphans, I learned quickly that my plight wasn't as unique as I had once thought. I was not alone; I was among friends.

By summer's end I was ready to give West Philly High another chance. I made friends, became active on the school paper, and worked my way up to editor-in-chief. In a short year and a half, I became an active member of the school. Once again I had broken through the wall that separated outsiders from insiders, even though I had developed an irrational fear that with every success comes failure.

In my senior year I switched all my courses so that I would be eligible, on graduation, to enter the Army Specialist Training Program (ASTP). Prerequisites for acceptance into the program were high concentrations of math, science and chemistry.

The ASTP was Secretary of War Henry Stimson's baby. The program was originally designed to accommodate 150,000 of the best and the brightest men. Those who entered the army in 1943 and passed the ASTP entrance exam would be given the rank and pay of a private and sent to college campuses around the country where they would receive an accelerated college education. Upon graduation they would be sent to Officers' Candidate School and then to the war zone. The army's logic in planning the program was to continually fill the officers' pipeline with bright, educated young men.[6]

To prepare myself for the qualifying examination, I devoted all my free time to study. I passed the entrance exam for ASTP, finished the school term, graduated with the class of 1943, and was ready to offer my services to the United States of America.

But before volunteering my services with Uncle Sam, I believed that another summer at S.G.F. was my due for working so hard on my ASTP certification.

With America at war, in the summer of 1943, filling the

post of Director of S.G.F. had been difficult. All the men who were physically fit were eligible for the draft. It was Sam G. Friedman himself, known as Uncle Brud to those who loved him, who recruited Jimmy Sax. Uncle Brud literally, physically brought him to camp to become the new director. Jimmy had previous experience in camp direction and Friedman knew that Jimmy would not be inducted because during his youth his brother had fired a BB gun in their home that had ricocheted off several walls and blinded Jimmy in one eye.

James Ezekiel Sax, a very proper, intelligent, warm human being, came into my life the day I arrived for my second summer at camp. He was proud of his middle name because he could trace his grandmother's Ezekiel family back to the 1700s, when Abraham Ezekiel founded what is now the second oldest synagogue in Great Britain. Jimmy was to become my mentor and a devoted friend, and I his protégé.

When I met Jim Sax he was a popular young bachelor active on the social scene. Prominent names such as Snellenburg, Gimbel and Wolf rolled off his tongue. He was the genealogist for "our crowd" in Philadelphia. I found it exciting just to listen to him, feeling that I was seeing Philadelphia society through a keyhole. I was thrilled when he unlocked that door and invited me to his family home for dinner in the Overbrook section of Philadelphia. Here at his family dwelling on Drexel Drive I first experienced "high society." Dinners were very formal. The table was adorned with flowers and set with Jimmy's Grandfather Sax's Tiffany sterling. The plates were of gold and white china, and delicious food arrived at each place through the services of Josephine the maid. Discussions at the table were lively and focused on current events. The table was always full of people; Jimmy's parents were seated at either end, and Jimmy had two brothers and a sister who added to the noise. Mrs. Sax was quite deaf and used a long, curved, tin ear trumpet. In order for her husband to converse with her he had to shout the length of the boisterous table, further increasing the decibel level.

Jimmy also introduced me to one of the pleasures of the elite, horseback riding in Fairmount Park. I had seen plenty of horses but I had never been on one in my life. Once I became accustomed to wrapping my legs around the equine and squeezing hard with my knees, I began to enjoy the experience.

When Jimmy arrived at S.G.F., I was assigned to the office to help him run the camp. I was seventeen, and Jimmy was my boss. If the truth were known, neither of us knew what we were doing that summer. But I am a quick learner, and by the following summer, Jimmy was still the director but I was managing the details and running the camp. Jimmy's genius was in his relationship with the campers.

At the end of my second summer at S.G.F., in the fall of 1943, I presented myself to the army induction center to join the ASTP. The interviewing sergeant reviewed each application. Then in a loud voice that everyone could hear, he barked, "Aaron, you're not a citizen of the United States. I can't let you into ASTP." With my tail between my legs, I left the induction center.

What was I to do now? I had finished high school, completed my delightful summer at S.G.F., and found myself back in Philadelphia with no definite plans.

It was my new friend, Jimmy Sax, who came to the rescue. Jimmy was on the board of directors of the Neighborhood Center in charge of youth activities; they needed a young man to staff the new Helen Teller Youth Center. If I wanted the job, it was mine.

The Neighborhood Center had been established in 1885 by a group of philanthropic Jewish women and by the 1940s had become a vital, lively institution serving the entire area. The organization, originally called The Young Women's Union, had been dedicated to the assimilation of the many Eastern European Jews who had settled in the South Philadelphia area. By the early 1940s the focus of the center had changed to become recreational and social. In 1942 the center established a teen-age youth center, the first in Philadelphia to do so. Departments of arts and crafts, golden age clubs and a variety of sports were also inaugurated, and the Neighborhood Players, a semi-professional group of actors, performed plays on weekends in what became known as the Neighborhood Playhouse.

I took the job and became employed part-time as host of the Helen Teller Youth Center. One of my assignments at the Neighborhood Center was to supervise the program in the youth lounge that was frequented by poor Jewish kids in trouble. I was to guide them along the straight and narrow. The lounge contained a pool table and a Ping-Pong table, and my job was to teach the kids how to play both. I became an avid pool player, but, there were times when I left part of my weekly salary on the pool table through my bets with the wayward kids. (I became the wayward supervisor rather than the advisor.) Wages earned for the next six months totaled $540.

The Neighborhood Center was known throughout the Philadelphia area for its powerful basketball team, which had won many awards in the Jewish Basketball League of

Philadelphia. One could always recognize basketball players who had trained at the N.C.; their shots at the basket would be long and low, never high. The reason was quite simple: The ceiling in the Neighborhood Center gym was extremely low, and if you wanted to shoot baskets, you had to keep your shots long and low. During the 1940s one player whose height helped him dominate the game was a young man named Julian A. Brodsky.

The Neighborhood Playhouse became well known, and many professional actors received their training there. One of the actresses was Sue Fleisher. In the 1940s a young, handsome naval ensign would patiently stand at the stage door waiting for Sue to finish rehearsals. After the war, she would marry the good-looking ensign, Ralph J. Roberts.

Isn't fate strange? Years later, Ralph Roberts, Julian Brodsky and I—all unknown to one another at the time— were to meet and become the founding fathers of a cable company. No doubt we rubbed elbows as we walked along the corridors of the center.

In September of 1943 Mrs. Myers sold her house, and I was on my own.

The Neighborhood Center had boarding rooms available for staff members to help them maintain close contact with the community, and I moved into one of these rooms. Frank, still a ward of the Association For Jewish Children, stayed in the foster home care program for another five years until he reached the age of eighteen. Although physically separated, Frank and I remained in close touch.

Even though our constant move from one foster home to another did not make for a secure, happy childhood, I learned one very important lesson: Children can adapt to almost any situation as long as they feel motivated and there is no physical harm.

Having been rejected from the ASTP, I wanted to continue my education, so I enrolled in Temple University's School of Liberal Arts, using money that I had saved from my work at the Neighborhood Center and my winnings at the pool table. I had just turned eighteen, ripe for the draft, but I was able to finish my first term at Temple and benefit from another summer at S.G.F. before I was drafted.

Alien or not, I received my induction notice from Uncle Sam in 1944. In retrospect, the officious sergeant's barking rejection a year earlier might well have saved my life. By the fall of 1943, the army had cut the Army Specialist Training Program from 150,000 men to 30,000. Most of the specialists ended up in rifle companies on the front lines in Europe just as the Battle of the Bulge was beginning. A disproportionately large percentage of these were either killed or wounded in action.[7]

In the fall of 1944, Uncle Sam inducted me into the United States Army.

5   *"You're in the army now"*

The fact that I was not an American citizen did not stop the U.S. Army from drafting me in the fall of 1944. With a shortage of field personnel, the army simply exercised its right to draft any able-bodied resident of the United States. When they saw from my induction papers that I was German, not American, I was ordered to raise my right hand and pledge allegiance to the United States of America. According to my induction papers I weighed 152 pounds, had brown eyes and brown hair and was only 5'7" tall.

I took my basic training at Fort Campbell, Kentucky, in December. After the required period of training (about which the less said the better), we were on our graduation march, colloquially known by the participants as the "survival march," when training was interrupted and we were ordered hurriedly back to camp. The Battle of the Bulge had begun and reinforcements were needed on the European front.

The Battle of the Bulge was the last German offensive of World War II. In mid-December 1944, as Allied forces advanced on Germany, Hitler launched a counterattack to repel Allied forces and retake the strategic Belgian seaport of Antwerp. Before the counterattack was halted, the Nazis had advanced thirty miles into Belgium, creating a bulge in the Allied lines. Allied strength prevailed and the German army slowly withdrew. By the end of January 1945, more than a million men had participated in the battle, with tens of thousands on both sides killed or wounded.

We crossed the Atlantic on the *Queen Mary*, which had been refurbished as a troop ship. On this crossing there was no one aboard to insist that I eat with the first-class passengers. We were in steerage, and I spent most of my time waiting in a food line so slow moving that dinner often became breakfast.

One incident aboard disturbed me greatly. A discussion ensued about the old anti-Semitic saw that the Jews never serve their country in case of war. We Jews tried in vain to point out that our presence clearly proved otherwise. But it was to no avail; once again we saw how anti-Semitism poisons the mind.

We landed in France in early February and were attached to the Ninth Army. I found myself in the Fifty-eighth Infantry Battalion, Eighth Armored Division, that was fighting its way across Belgium to the German border. As infantry personnel in full battle fatigues, we traveled in long columns of halftracks, trucks equipped with tractor treads at the rear. A single tank preceded each of these columns of all-terrain vehicles. The German anti-tank corps had turned their eighty-eight millimeter anti-aircraft guns into high-velocity anti-tank weapons that could penetrate tank armor. To be assigned to the lead tank was considered a death sentence. Should we hear a shot, our modus operandi was to jump out of our halftrack, lie in the gully on the side of the road, and hope that our lead tank knocked out the enemy position.

At ease in 1944 — U.S. 33951898.

During one of these skirmishes we lost our squad leader. It was the first time that I had seen one of my buddies killed, and I was gloomy for days.

This description of crossing the Rhine is excerpted from my journal written shortly after the event. I was only nineteen years old at the time, thinking in my native tongue but writing in my second language. Fifty-five years later I am extracting with slight revisions:

We left Grefrath on March 2, 1945, several days after the Ninth Army crossed the Rhine. We crossed the river that same night; it was a most thrilling and frightening experience. There were four of us in the Major's jeep: the Major, his driver, and two interpreters.

At midnight we made our crossing using a two-way pontoon bridge that had been constructed by the Corps of Engineers. It was an ingenious span for which the Corps had received a citation. The Germans tried all night to destroy it. Their newly developed jet-propelled fighters were in the air in great numbers. It was a dark night. Had it not been for the searchlights and the tracer bullets we could not have followed the pandemonium that went on in the sky. The fire from our "ack ack" guns covered the whole area, setting up a constant field of fire. I don't know if you have ever seen tracer bullets. They look like firecrackers. Actually, a tracer bullet is one with an added chemical that gives off a brilliant red flame when fired and permits the gunner to follow the trajectory of the bullet. Our anti-aircraft guns were set up on the west bank and produced a steady stream of fire traveling across the dark sky. Now and then a brilliant beam from a searchlight would cut through the darkness seeking out the remnants of the German Luftwaffe. The scene produced a brilliant spectacle.

Once on the east bank of the Rhine, our troops fought

hard for every inch of ground they covered. It was difficult combat and we lost a lot of men. I could never understand why the Germans didn't surrender. They had obviously lost the war at this point. They were out of fuel, ammunition was running low, the Luftwaffe was in shambles; but that didn't seem to matter. They continued to fight.

Near the end of the war, I was transferred to Military Intelligence because of my fluency in German. One of my duties was to set up a military government that included local Germans whose careers were not tainted by Nazism or membership in the Nazi party. When one listened to the Germans' responses to our questions, one was convinced that there was no Nazi party. No one wanted to admit membership. Our officer in charge of military affairs became increasingly frustrated.

However, we finally did find our Nazi. During a routine search we discovered a hidden SS uniform, and its owner admitted to being a Nazi. My commander called me into his office and said, "Aaron, take this son of a bitch down into the basement and torture him." I took the victim downstairs. Then I tried to figure out what to do.

What did an American Jewish boy from West Philly know about torture?

The only thing that came to mind was to bark commands, marching him back and forth in the cellar. To persuade my superior that I was doing my job, I told my victim to march into the wall before turning around and to scream loudly as he did so. His wife heard the commotion and came down to see her husband running into the wall and screaming. Now I found myself surrounded by a screaming storm trooper and his wailing wife. I wondered how I could extricate myself from this charade.

Finally I called a halt to the marching, and my role of "torturer" came to an end with little damage. Only later did any of the participants remember that army rules strictly forbade physical harm to prisoners.

While our front-line companies were fighting and advancing, my section was two or three towns behind, setting up military governments. On entering a town we would first distribute pamphlets ordering all civilians off the street for the next forty-eight hours and, next, post Eisenhower's "Allied Policy" in the town square. If time permitted we would choose a new *Buergermeister* or mayor, and a police force to run the town. From the latter part of March 1945 until the last week in April, we secured twenty-one towns.

It was just dumb luck that I was one of the first soldiers to come across the secret German army research laboratory that developed torpedoes and rockets. It had been under the supervision of Wernher von Braun, who had developed the rockets that fell indiscriminately on the civilian population of England, killing thousands.

Before being whisked away from the site by our security people, I had a chance to talk with one of the German scientists. I was appalled at what I learned; the scientist was interested only in the scientific results of his experiments. To what use the finished product was put was not his concern. As long as he was in the good graces of his superiors, nothing else mattered. When the Allies arrived, this scientist was happy to relinquish his laboratory, records and all the models that were being worked on even though specific orders had been given to him to destroy everything. After the war, these same German scientists received prime positions in our space program. Peace also makes strange bedfellows!

The biggest town we secured was Braunschweig. We

entered just two days after the infantry had captured the town. For the first time I saw the effects of war on a German city: The center of the town was destroyed and one street looked like the next, full of stones, bricks, broken furniture and burned-out buildings.

One incident seems funny in retrospect. It was at a time when the Ninth Army was rushing across Germany to beat the Russians into Berlin. Knowing that I spoke German, our battalion commander awakened me in the middle of the night to lead our group to Berlin. Try as I might, I was not able to persuade him that I had a terrible sense of direction. To lead our group to Berlin was completely beyond my capabilities.

Our commander would have none of it. He expected his commands to be obeyed; I would guide our unit of the Ninth Army across Germany, period. It didn't take long for him to realize what a mistake he had made. Within five minutes I was lost; I didn't have the foggiest notion as to north, south, east or west, much less the direction in which Berlin lay. Then I happened to notice a gas station that had re-opened. Speaking German, I asked one of the attendants for a map, and with the aid of a tourist map, I helped speed the Ninth Army toward Berlin.

I was particularly disturbed by what the Germans did to the slave labor camp inmates. This is another excerpt from my journal:

As the Allied forces advanced, the retreating Germans would release the slave laborers from their internment. The Wehrmacht would open up the camps behind their lines and drive these pathetic, starved hordes of people into our lines.

These masses of stunned people would clog the roads,

steal, loot, and generally terrorize the countryside. Like a herd of cattle they roamed through the country, one group followed by another, no one knowing where to go. At times we had to stop them because they were heading back into the German lines.

It was an impossible job to try to gather them up and bring them back to their assigned transportation vehicles; they had suffered too much in similar vehicles at the hands of the Germans. It was the U.S. policy to send these former slave laborers back to their country of origin, and we were finally able to organize them for transportation back to their respective countries. The Jews among them objected.

When the first trainload, consisting of Polish Gentiles and Jews, arrived in Poland, their Polish compatriots had murdered all the Jews. The U.S. government immediately changed its policy.

The Germans did not unconditionally surrender until May 8, 1945, and for the five weeks from April 22 until June 8, our unit, S 5, acted as the army of occupation. The first town we administered was Sessen, a town of 15,000. Before we arrived in Sessen, another Allied outfit had set up a city administration. After two days of investigation, which included mixing with the local people, talking to the supposed anti-Nazis, and looking through the city records, we became convinced that the present *Buergermeister* and his staff were a Nazi clique. It was our duty to find another administration. We discovered that the majority of the people were fed up with Nazism and, if asked, would point out the anti-Nazis of the town. I found that cooperation was a give-and-take affair; when the people saw that we were fair in our dealings with them, they reciprocated in kind. Playing the conquering hero didn't work. With the help of the townspeople, we did find a new *Buergermeister* and a staff to help him, and they performed admirably.

By the middle of June I found myself in Paris awaiting re-assignment to the Asian front. The Far East was the last place any of us wanted to go. We were convinced that, having survived one war in Europe, we could not rely on that same luck a second time. But the feared reassignment never materialized, and two months later, as I was strolling along the Champs-Élysées, a headline at the newsstand caught my eye: A U.S. bomber, the *Enola Gay,* had dropped an atomic bomb on Hiroshima. The date was August 6, 1945.

On September 2, Japan formally surrendered to the Allies. Within two months I was back in the States.

Wages had been frozen throughout the war, but now workers wanted their fair share of the profits. It was no longer a case of patriotism for the war effort; labor was fed up. Some 200,000 meatpackers went out on strike. In Pittsburgh 3,500 electric company workers went out, causing plant closings that affected 100,000 workers. The glass workers struck, General Electric went out, and the telephone company followed. Even the coffinmakers wanted their fair share.[8]

President Truman had his hands full. Adding to his problems were the twelve million men and women in uniform who would be coming home and demanding jobs. Swelling the workforce with those numbers would be disastrous. Keeping some of the troops in uniform might alleviate part of the problem. As battle-experienced soldiers we were told we were being trained to control conflicts arising from strikes; in truth we were being trained as strike-breakers.

It was almost a year before I would be mustered out of

service. On June 26, 1946, I was honorably discharged from the army as a technician fifth grade from Company B, Fifty-eighth Armored Infantry Battalion.

I was twenty-and-a-half years old, with $363.62 in severance pay in my pocket, when I left the United States Army. My severance pay was enough for me to return to Philadelphia, make arrangements to continue my college education, and pay for my travel expenses to Collegeville for summer camp at S.G.F. My teen-age years were behind me. It was 1946, and another phase of my life was about to unfold. I was looking forward to some kind of positive change.

6 *Gerrie*

One of the most significant pieces of American wartime legislation was the G.I. Bill, or Servicemen's Readjustment Act, signed into law by President Roosevelt on June 22, 1944.

Under this act the government subsidized tuition, fees, books, and living expenses incurred by veterans while they were in school. Roosevelt's rationale, apart from that of obligation, was that this further education would benefit both veterans and the nation and would serve as a cushion against unemployment. The ex-soldiers were allowed to select the educational institution of their choice, and the respective institutions were free to admit only those students who met their individual admissions requirements. The effects of increased enrollment were significant; more teachers had to be hired, new classrooms and laboratories built, and housing for students had to be increased. These new students were older than the usual college age, and they came to learn. More than seven million vets nationwide took advantage of program; 250,000 were African Americans. Socially, the ramifications were enormous: People who would have been denied advancement due to their socioeconomic circumstance were able to move into the mainstream of the American middle class.

In the fall term of 1946, thanks to the G.I. Bill, I enrolled in Temple University in Philadelphia with a major in economics, as one of thousands of veterans who attended Temple.

The two blocks of Broad Street between Columbia Avenue and Norris Street defined my student world. As I exited the subway, the newsstand at the northwest corner of Broad and Columbia Avenue was my eyes and ears of the world and helped shape my philosophy. I picked the liberal publications, *PM, The Nation,* and *Harper's* magazine. My next stop was Linton's Restaurant where food rolled out of the kitchen on a conveyor belt. A fifty-cent breakfast of one scrambled egg, buttered bread with jelly, and a brown betty —a baked apple pudding—supplied me with my sustenance.

Across the street from Linton's was Wilkie Buick, a car agency that sported the latest models; it fed my daydreams stimulated by the tempting refrain, "Wouldn't you really rather have a Buick?" After breakfast, my meal for the day, I walked the short distance north on Broad Street for a full day of study at Temple.

As for my extracurricular activities, no one had ever accused me of being a Casanova. Women were a mystery to me. I was extremely self-conscious of my accent, my lack of status, and my poverty. My contact with women had been strictly platonic and I found women four or five years older less threatening. I still feel embarrassed to remember the extent of my discomfort: Before I graduated from West Philadelphia High, a number of parties were planned for the upcoming graduates. I was dying to be invited to one of them. I was, and the party was held at a house on Germantown Avenue in Philadelphia. I arrived in plenty of time to join in the festivities. There was just one problem; I could not bring myself to go inside. Instead, I walked up to the door, turned in panic, and walked back to the street. After a few trips around the outside of the house to buoy my courage, I left, too shy to enter.

During my second term at Temple, I met a charming young coed who was destined to become my best friend for a lifetime. Geraldine Stone was a spellbinder. I had always pictured myself as a sober, joyless outsider. Gerrie Stone was the antithesis; she was the life of the party, a free spirit with great charm, an English major who loved to dance and sing. She was a very sunny person.

What a difference Gerrie made!

Gerrie and I attended the same class in mathematics. Math was not Gerrie's forte; she would much rather paint, dance and sing. She asked me to help her with her homework, and I didn't have to be asked twice. We found ourselves enjoying each other's company and we began to date on an intermittent basis. Gerrie was much sought after and had many invitations; I found myself standing in a long line.

The first time Gerrie invited me to dinner, I accepted her invitation readily. I learned on my arrival that her mother, the cook in the family, happened to be out of town. That left Gerrie to prepare and cook the meal for her father as well as for our mutual friend, Janet Fuhrman, who had introduced the two of us, and me. Gerrie remembers that dinner as a disaster; the beans were burned and the chicken was overcooked. That was Gerrie's reaction. I could not have cared less about the dinner; it was the cook that I was after.

At the time, I was renting a room on Thirteenth Street from two little old ladies. My room was small and the bed occupied most of the space, with little room for a bureau and a chair, but it was all I could afford and to me it was quite adequate. On the landing of the stairs going up to my room was a very large statue of the Virgin Mary that I would greet respectfully as I passed. Any friend visiting did a double-take, not knowing whether they were passing a life-sized doll or a real person. My first night in the house had been memorable. Getting into bed I felt a large lump between the sheet and the mattress. On examination, I discovered a large crucifix had been put there. Were the ladies trying to convert me?

With Gerrie's help, my Americanization went into full gear. Gerrie restored my self-respect, which had been shattered by the catastrophes of the Holocaust. She helped me overcome my discomfort and insecurity with women; she was the teacher and I the willing student. In long nightly sessions at a neighborhood bar we would learn about each other. As we talked, we discovered that our personalities complemented each other. I was falling in love.

While I listened to Beethoven's Ninth Symphony, Gerrie would memorize the lyrics of every popular song and the arrangement of every new jazz piece. Her favorite entertainer was Josh White, who drove her wild when he sang "My Big Brass Bed"; all she would have needed was a wink in her direction. Gerrie has a wonderful ear for music. She loved to play the piano, sing to the accompaniment of her guitar, and dance. After marriage Gerrie would teach "Dancercize," an aerobic form of modern dance, and would develop a devoted following throughout the Philadelphia area.

Thanksgiving dinner was a family affair at the home of the Stones. Although their immediate family was not large, they would always expand their festive table with good friends. Hirsch and Trixie Stalberg were invited in 1947 for a specific reason: I had been courting Gerrie for a few months, and the Stalbergs were to help decide if I was good enough for their host's lovely daughter. The Stalbergs gave the Stones the thumbs-up sign before leaving, *Gott sei Dank* (thank God!). And that's how Hirsch Stalberg became the *Shadkhan* (matchmaker).

Gerrie's father was not pleased. Edward Stone was a well-known Philadelphia attorney. During the Great Depression when clients walked out of, rather than into, a lawyer's office, Ed Stone gave up his law practice to become city hall editor of the *Philadelphia Record.* He later returned to his law practice, and among his honorary duties was serving as rotating editor of *The Shingle,* a free weekly paper published by the legal community. (Many years later, when my son Jud finished law school and was waiting for an interview at local law office, he picked up a magazine that featured the celebration of the fiftieth anniversary of *The Shingle.* To his surprise, there was a picture of his late grandfather, my father-in-law.)

Marriage to a penniless German refugee wasn't exactly what the Stones had in mind for their beautiful, popular daughter, but the harder they pressed the more determined their daughter became. In the spring of 1948, Gerrie told her mother in no uncertain terms, "Dan is the man."

Gerrie and I became engaged in June of 1948, and that summer Gerrie used to borrow the family car to make the trip to Collegeville to visit me on weekends at S.G.F.

One of my fellow counselors and my good friend, Bill Besser, claims that one night I crept into his cabin and stole his favorite blue blanket. He insists his blanket disappeared

*On our wedding day:
Gerrie and Dan,
December 26, 1948.*

into the woods with "the lovesick couple," and he has been looking for it ever since. Gerrie and I insist that the story is apocryphal.

After a short, torrid engagement we were married on December 26, 1948, just six months after our engagement. I was a sophomore at Temple and Gerrie, having completed her undergraduate studies, was studying for her teaching certification. I would be twenty-three in less than a month, my bride a year younger.

It is a Jewish custom that the bride's family underwrites the wedding and the groom is responsible for the honorarium to the rabbi who performs the ceremony. Knowing nothing of this custom, I had spent my last ten dollars buying a wedding necktie at Morville's, a fancy men's haberdashery on Walnut Street.

After the ceremony, Gerrie's father sidled up to me and whispered, "The rabbi needs his fifty dollars."

I replied, "Tell him, so do I."

Ed Stone loaned me the money. Our wedding was saved, but the episode provided my father-in-law with further evidence that his daughter faced a difficult future.

Gerrie and I did not plan to start a family for quite some time, but we must have changed our minds. Five years later, in 1953, Erika was born; Jimmy followed in January of 1955, Kenny eleven months later, and Jud two years after that. We had three kids in diapers at one time. Then Alison was born in 1961.

Looking back more than fifty years later, and having two daughters of my own, I can empathize with the Stones and their fears of their daughter marrying a young man who was still in school and then starting a family so quickly. Even so, my relationship with Gerrie's parents developed into one of admiration and mutual trust. We became very close friends. In a way, Ed and Marie became the parents I never had.

On the day Gerrie and I were married, a photograph was taken of the two of us. It has hung over my desk ever since. Our comments to each other when we first saw the picture said it all:

Gerrie said, "You look sexy and thoughtful."

I said, "You also look sexy and thoughtful."

We were off to a good start.

7 *Hooky cop*

Gerrie's father was correct; we didn't have much money to live on, and our lifestyle certainly didn't include any frills. But it mattered little; we were in love, enjoying each other's company, and we were building a solid foundation to our marriage. I was in college, and thanks to Uncle Sam my basic expenses were covered. To help supplement our income Gerrie went to work full time and I took weekend jobs.

One of my jobs was as a waiter in the Jewish Waiter's Union, which supplied staff to local Jewish caterers. For a weekend's work, the pay was $25, a generous amount in those days. The Union was very popular among area students, and many a Philadelphia doctor or lawyer could not have gotten through graduate school without those jobs.

It took time and experience to learn how to balance a full tray of eight dinners, but after a few nights, I had no problem with my balancing act and, fortunately, no mishaps. But what I could not get used to was one caterer's SOP (standard operating procedure). After the guests had finished dinner and I had cleared the table, I found my way to the kitchen blocked by the wife of the caterer. It was her job to cull any leftover chicken from the customer's plates. These gleanings would be used to make the next day's chicken salad.

And then there was the flaming jubilee dessert ceremony, a ritual that featured ice cream bathed in a sauce of liqueur and then ignited. The waiter, with gusto, would place the flaming dish in front of the guests and with great drama put out the flames. However, if a table was unruly or unkind, or if the guests indicated there would be little tip, our retribution was to walk away from the flaming jubilee and let the fire blaze to the consternation of the guests, none of whom knew how to extinguish the fire.

It was Gerrie's steady job that took the edge off our subsistence lifestyle. Gerrie worked for the Board of Education as a truant officer, colloquially called "a hooky cop." It was an emotionally taxing and difficult job, but my dear wife stuck with it for four and a half years, enabling me to finish my studies at Temple and pursue graduate studies later.

Gerrie's assigned area stretched from Broad Street north to Diamond Street, south to Lehigh Avenue and east to Kensington. The multiethnic clients who made up the population were hard-working poor people living in cramped rowhouses that were heated by coal. Many had no indoor plumbing. Employment—what little there was—was found in local factories such as Bayuk Cigars, the home of the "Phillies" cigar, Stetson Hats, and the remaining mills that hadn't moved to the South to take advantage of cheaper wages. Breweries, too, were scattered throughout the area with names such as Schmidt's, Gretz and Esslinger.

It was into this setting that my remarkable wife pursued her rounds; she understood what was meant by "the dark brown smell of poverty."

Gerrie well remembers the terrible conditions:

"I was looking for a truant child in the Kensington area. The house the family occupied was small, three rooms stacked one on top of another and known as a 'father, son and holy ghost' house. The father I called on didn't look directly at me as I questioned him about his truant child. As he finally turned I could see that he was wearing a scarf around his neck. When I asked why his child wasn't in school, he carefully unwrapped the scarf and to my horror revealed a fresh knife wound showing that his throat had been slashed from ear to ear. His only comment was, 'I don't have much time for my kid these days.' I turned and left quickly.

"Another frightening experience was my trip to see a family whose child had not appeared in school for several days. I entered their second-floor flat to be greeted by the husband who said I should be talking with his Mrs. Not knowing that his spouse was mentally unbalanced, I followed him into the bedroom. To my shock, his wife jumped over the bed, flying at me like an attack dog. Luckily, the husband intervened so I could back away. I was terrified. I recommended that they be sent to court and let the juvenile justice department handle it.

"Making my rounds, I wore a heavy green gabardine coat belted at the waist, sporting a fake fur collar. I wore sensible oxford walking shoes that laced up the front, and under my arm I carried a manila envelope full of case histories. I looked like a social worker, and everyone in the neighborhood thought I was one.

"A popular excuse for not attending school was sickness, an excuse that had to be authenticated by a doctor. Unfortunately, some unethical physicians in the neighborhood would sign an excuse note just to collect a fee. Some children in my caseload had a raft of doctor's excuses, and I wondered how long an 'upper respiratory infection' could last.

"Children who had no shoes had the saddest excuse for truancy. Shoes were available through various social agencies and I would give the parents a list, hoping that they would follow through.

"Many of my cases were sad but I felt that with the help of the court system, I could make a difference for the children. In one house an eight-year-old was taking care of three of his siblings while his mother was at the corner bar, drinking and carousing with men in the neighborhood. It was obvious to me why this child wasn't in school. This situation necessitated a court order to remove the children from their mother and place them in foster homes.

"The agency's policy on pregnancy was strictly enforced; employment was terminated after the first trimester. My supervisor, Dr. John Calhoun, a huge man who was scary as hell, followed this policy to the letter. So, when I became pregnant with Erika in 1952, I was petrified that I would lose my job. We needed the money, so as my stomach began to protrude I would camouflage myself with big sweaters and jackets. My morning sickness was exacerbated by the coal dust odors from the homes I visited; the fumes were so awful that many times I just couldn't stand it. I remember the time I left my client's house as fast as I could, leaned against a telephone pole, and said to myself, 'Oh please don't throw up here.' Getting onto the trolley to get home was no better because my travel time coincided with rush hour for the factory workers. The smell of unwashed bodies would force me off the trolley and I would walk the rest of the way home.

"In my seventh month, with much trepidation, I walked into John Calhoun's office to let him know that I had to quit because I was pregnant. 'Yes,' he said, 'I have known it for months.' I guess he wasn't such a bad guy after all."

Gerrie's job was only one of the uncertainties that she coped with throughout our early years.

During our married life at school, we lived in an apartment on Park Avenue, one stop south of Temple University on the Broad Street subway. It was a short walk from our living quarters to the Susquehanna-Dauphin subway stop. This apartment was worlds away from a Park Avenue apartment in New York; it was in a converted home that was in constant disrepair. We slept in the small living room and dining room area on a hand-me-down bed that one of our relatives had given us. The kitchen was in a closet, and for unwanted guests we had our share of cockroaches. Our only expenditure was an antique breakfast table that enabled us to enjoy our meals sitting down. We are still using the table today.

But the size and condition of the apartment mattered little. We were constantly visited by friends and had a wonderful time there. In 1949, television was in its infancy and not available as the diversion it is today. For entertainment one had to be creative, so we entertained ourselves by listening in on our telephone party line. A party line, which let three or four parties share one telephone line, substantially reduced the individual cost. The only drawback of this system was that everyone could listen in to the conversation of everyone else. In our case, we shared a party line with a young "lady of the street" whose clientele lived in Chinatown. Her conversations with her trade were most amusing and enlightening, and when our friends found out about this, it was amazing how our Friday night visitations increased.

During our first summer as a couple I decided that instead of my returning to S.G.F. alone, we should try to obtain a summer job together. With my Jewish Union waiter experience under my belt, I answered an ad for waiter at Camp Nockamoxin, a camp for adults located in the Borscht Belt of the Catskills. We were both pleased when our application for summer employment as waiter and waitress was accepted. As naive youngsters we were pleased to have summer jobs, but we should have done our homework.

Unknown to us, the owner of Camp Nockamoxin promised male companionship to women guests who attended his camp. To meet that obligation, the proprietor advertised in the media promising each prospective female camper a "young man available for companionship." Everyone else knew the meaning of those code words and had renamed the camp "Camp knock 'em up." The studs would arrive Friday evening in their fancy convertibles, eye the line of young women guests, and select their companions for the weekend.

Gerrie and I worked terribly hard serving five meals a day, including a midnight snack. Dead tired, we would retire to our room and literally drop into bed. There was only one problem; our room was located over the dance band, which played throughout the early morning hours.

My wife was the only female waiter, and when the fellow waiters and the cook started eyeing her—and, even worse, asking to date her—I had had enough. The season was only half over, but we were out of there.

As an antidote to our poisonous month at camp we decided, before going back to Philadelphia, to stay a few nights in New York City at an inexpensive hotel on Times Square where we shared the bathroom facilities with twenty other guests. This was a treat? After the summer of 1949, Gerrie wondered if her parents' fears weren't justified.

Back at Temple, my studies reflected my increasingly liberal philosophy. Whether because of my own history or of my inherent personality, I wanted to be a positive force for change, making society more responsive to the needs of all the people. My politics were left of the Democratic Party. The friends I made, the courses I chose, and the organizations I joined all directed my interest to the socialist movement in the United States. I worked for the Progressive Party, whose presidential candidate was Henry Wallace, vice-president during Franklin Roosevelt's third term.

At Temple I was fortunate to have a teacher who left a profound mark on me. Dr. Barrows Dunham, head of the philosophy department of which he was the lone member, had just published his first book, *Man Against Myth,* in which he defended his belief that there is only one side to any question, and that is the right side. A professed Marxist, his convictions were tested when Joe McCarthy called him before the Senate committee on un-American activities. He took the Fifth Amendment and was promptly fired from Temple by its newly elected president. It was not one of Temple's finest hours, but for us students it was a lesson in courage, conviction and commitment. To Temple's credit, Dr. Dunham was eventually reinstated.

Although there were many veterans' organizations to join, the largest being the American Legion, I chose the more liberal American Veterans Committee (AVC), founded in 1944 by a group of idealistic servicemen and women in uniform. Charles Bolte articulated the AVC's philosophy in his book *The New Veteran* which spelled out a "citizens first, veterans second" point of view. AVC was a forerunner in the fight to integrate the armed forces. Within a year of joining I became chairman of the Temple University chapter. In its early days the AVC survived an attempted takeover by the Communist Party, and fifty years later it continues to devote its energies to liberal causes. On the international front, AVC works with the United Nations toward peaceful resolution of conflicts. When President Reagan decided to visit Bitburg, Germany, where German and Nazi soldiers were laid to rest, AVC was the first veteran's organization to protest, believing the president's visit was an insult to all victims of the Nazi scourge. Even with a small membership, the AVC continues to serve the liberal conscience in national affairs and is a vital force in international efforts to create a just and peaceful world.

As graduation from Temple became more and more of a reality, I got down to the serious task of finding employment. As was my custom, I decided to do this alone, with no outside help. After much soul searching, I chose advertising agencies as my first target. I knew that I wrote well and with ease, and hadn't I been editor-in-chief of the West Philadelphia High School paper? It all seems so naive now.

Every liberal arts school graduate could have submitted the same resume. I listed all my part-time jobs at Lit Brothers, Wanamaker's, Bond's Clothing (the clothing store that offered two pair of pants with any suit), my waiter's experience and my employment at the Thirtieth Street post office during the Christmas holidays. I did not mention that I came very close to being fired from my job at Bond's.

I had worked at Bond's while in high school, advancing to head the department that sold men's slacks. In those days a salesman did it all: interested the customers in the product, sold the slacks and measured for the correct length. Measuring was performed with a tape that was placed carefully in a gentleman's crotch and extended down to the shoe line. One day I saw the announcement that Bond's was adding women's slacks to their stores. When I sold my first pair of slacks to a woman, I proceeded to measure the young lady the way I had been taught. She let out the appropriate scream, and I was almost fired. No one had informed me that women's measurements were taken from the hip down.

I sent out a hundred letters to ad agencies and other potential employers, requesting an interview and enclosing my resume. I waited . . . and waited . . . and waited. Not a single reply. So I decided to visit those agencies that had received my resume, appearing unannounced. The conversation would always be the same: I would ask to see the president, and inevitably, an officious secretary would block my entrance.

"Does he know you?" she would ask.

"Yes."

"How?"

"He received a letter from me."

"Does it pertain to employment?" (This question always created a sick feeling in the pit of my stomach, which haunts me to this day, every time I see a want ad.)

"We won't see anyone without an appointment," continued "Miss Officious."

"I am available at his convenience."

"We are too busy now to make appointments."

By now I was confused as to who he was, who we were, and who I was!

I gave up in despair. It was my version of Catch-22, and I never forgot the frustration of this demeaning experience.

Later in my career, I always maintained an open door policy for job interviews.

It was from my friend Marty Foreman that I sought advice. A long and serious discussion ensued, and we concluded that law school was the right direction. Money for our education was not a problem, for both of us, with the help of our wives, had saved enough money for future studies. We asked other friends for counsel. But they all repeated the same "party line": You can't be a successful lawyer without the proper contacts. No one had to tell us that Marty and I were poor boys who had no contacts of our own; we were vividly aware of that fact. They all dissuaded us from becoming attorneys. Marty shifted his horizons to sociology. I never even considered asking my father-in-law for help.

I decided to escape the employment "killing field" and return to school. Later, after more schooling, I would again seek employment. Gerrie fully supported this decision, even though it meant two extra years of work for her and a delay in starting our family.

With these plans in mind I applied to both the University of Pennsylvania and Cornell. As an honor student, I was accepted at both institutions. It became only a matter of choosing which one to attend.

My trip to Ithaca to investigate Cornell University is best left to Gerrie's description:

"When Dan was asked by the Cornell Graduate School of Labor Relations to travel to the university for an interview, I went with him to see if I could find employment for the years that he would be in school. It was the middle of winter, and by the time we arrived at our destination we found the area covered with snow. Coming from milder Philadelphia, I had not thought to pack the proper winter clothing. The only shoes I had were my high heels, worn because I wanted to look nice for my interviews. While Dan went to his interview I traipsed the city seeking a job, the snow soaking through my thin soles.

"Having been an English major, I tried the local radio station only to be asked if I could write 'sustaining or interval ads.' My blank look provoked the interviewer to say, 'Why don't you go get a book on radio, read it, and when you've done so come back and see me?'

"Every night, cold, wet and discouraged, I cried to go home to Philadelphia. I wasn't much help to Dan. The only job available was in the school of agriculture counting chickens as they passed through an opening in a wire fence. I remember thinking to myself, 'Thank God they aren't fruit flies.' After a few nights of wetting our pillows with my tears, we decided that the University of Pennsylvania would satisfy our needs much better than Cornell. Father was pleased: He had hoped that we would remain in Philadelphia."

Having made the decision, we returned to Temple so that I could finish my undergraduate program.

Temple University played an important role in our lives and holds a special place in my heart. It was at Temple that I met my Gerrie. We both graduated, she with a degree in English, I with high honors in economics. In the years to come, our daughter Erika would obtain her nursing degree from Temple and our son, Jud, a degree in law. *Dayenu!* (It would have been enough.) Then many years later, in 1994, I received Temple University's Diamond Achievement Award, an annual award created to "highlight the College's most successful graduates and provide current undergraduate students with an affirmation that a degree in Liberal Arts will provide a solid foundation for any and all career aspirations."

When I accepted the Diamond Achievement Award, I recalled that one of my Temple classmates was John Bunting, who became president of the First Pennsylvania Bank. He would often identify his alma mater as "Temple, Oh," because whenever a business associate asked what college he attended, and John replied, "Temple," the rejoinder would inevitably be, "Oh!" (As part of a less stodgy industry, that's a prejudice I never faced.) And so, three members of my family—my wife, our son and our daughter—all Temple alumni, like to say, "We went to Temple. Yea."

8 *"Nearly everybody reads it"*

Upon my graduation from Temple, Gerrie and I moved to Center City, Philadelphia, which in the early 1950s was a community of artists, long before it became a fashionable place to live. We found an apartment at Ninth and Clinton Streets in a home owned by a widow, Madame Portnoff. Her husband had been a famous Philadelphia artist, and every time she mentioned his name she would point to a jar on the mantel. It finally dawned on us that she was pointing to Portnoff's ashes.

We lived on the second floor of Madame Portnoff's converted mansion. The third floor, with its double-height ceilings and northern light, had been her husband's studio and it attracted a steady stream of artists who would stay until their rent money ran out. One of these artists was a rather odd chap whom we could hear pace back and forth all night creating his newest work. Every morning he would come down with the same sculpture—a head of Christ encircled by a fluorescent halo on an electrified wooden base—that he would try to sell door-to-door as a bedroom lamp. Needless to say, he quickly ran out of rent money. We felt we had moved to the left bank of the Seine; it was a far cry from our ersatz Park Avenue abode.

We would leave early in the morning, Gerrie for her work as a "hooky cop" and I as a student at the University of Pennsylvania. I was enrolled in the Liberal Arts College, pursuing a master's degree in finance, with a concentration in economics and journalism. We enjoyed our bohemian life. These were happy days. Every Friday night, our friends would meet us at Horn and Hardart's Ninth and Chestnut Streets automat to discuss the problems of the world. We had a special table and the discussions were always lively and to the left of liberal.

At Penn, the theory of economics was undergoing a great change, evolving from a social science to a more mathematical science. The new ideas were based on supply-and-demand curves, calculus, and an in-depth knowledge of statistics. I was not a supply-side economist; for me, economics dealt with the fair distribution of income. My heroes were the teachers who refused to surrender to the changes which, I felt, were just fads. To me, economics was based on the philosophies of Karl Marx and Friedrich Engels, Immanuel Kant and Georg Hegel. I admired those teachers who continued to treat economics as a social science.

One of my heroes was Professor George W. Taylor of the Wharton School at the University of Pennsylvania. He had acquired a national reputation during World War II as chairman of the National War Labor Board under President Franklin D. Roosevelt, and he taught labor relations through anecdotes of those events of which he had first-hand knowledge. Having won national fame and respect by negotiating settlements of strikes to maintain labor peace through the post-World War II era, he advocated less reliance on legal measures and more on bargaining to settle management differences. He regarded the law's machinery to achieve equitable settlements as important as its enforcement provisions. In his teachings and writings, as well as his work as a labor mediator and arbitrator, Dr. Taylor stressed the rights of the public over the narrow self-interests of the disputing parties. But at the same time he stressed the worker's right to strike as the ultimate tool that forced settlement.

"There is too much talk about the right to strike and too little about the purpose of strikes and whether they serve their purpose," he said. "But what is really thrilling is when representatives of labor and management finally come to an agreement and realize the immense satisfaction of having created order out of conflict. I think that's the essence of democracy."[9]

I was intrigued by Dr. Taylor's theory that the very groups that most opposed and hated President Franklin D. Roosevelt were saved by his New Deal. Taylor strongly believed that had there been no New Deal, a revolution well might have occurred in this country against the upper class.

Before his death in 1972, George W. Taylor would serve five presidents: first as Roosevelt's chairman of the National War Labor Board; next, as chairman of the Wage Stabilization Board in the Truman administration during the Korean conflict; and then, under President Dwight D. Eisenhower, as chairman of the Board of Inquiry during the 1959 steel strike. President John F. Kennedy would appoint him to the President's Advisory Committee on Labor Management Policy, where he would continue to serve under President Lyndon B. Johnson.

My two years at Penn passed quickly, and before I knew

Dr. George W. Taylor served five presidents and mentored many students. In 1952, he helped me put my freshly minted master's degree to work.

it I was again on a job search, only this time with more impressive credentials. It was 1952.

Finding a job was as difficult as before. The discussions that Marty and I had had about contacts as a way to climb the slippery ladder of success had not been forgotten. This time, I was going to learn the art of networking. This was troublesome for me, for I had always been a private person, and asking for help did not come easily, but if it took contacts to get a job, by God, I would make contacts.

With my background in journalism and economics, it was logical that I start working for a newspaper. My first candidate for a contact was George W. Taylor. Although most students were intimidated by his national stature, he was easily approachable, and I would regularly visit him for a follow-up discussion of his lecture of the day. One day Dr. Taylor called me into his office and asked if I would be interested in serving as assistant to Joseph A. Livingston, the writer of a syndicated column that appeared in four hundred newspapers around the country and financial editor of Philadelphia's most important daily newspaper, the *Evening Bulletin,* whose slogan was "Nearly everybody reads the *Bulletin.*"

Would I ever!

Dr. Taylor arranged a meeting with J. A. Livingston, who offered me a job as a financial writer after a five-minute interview, saying, "Anyone who is good enough for George Taylor is good enough for me."

The next day I reported to work at the *Bulletin* as an assistant to J. A. Livingston.

My title as financial writer did not really describe my job, a lowly "gofer" for *Bulletin* reporters. In my first assignment as copy boy, I monitored the AP and UP wires as stories moved across the Teletype, and then delivered the appropriate articles to the reporters.

Joseph A. Livingston was the dean of Philadelphia journalists. He was a sharp-eyed, patrician-looking professional who turned his outstanding intellect and journalistic ability to writing about financial and economic affairs. His writing was renowned among his peers: He crafted each sentence as a diamond cutter polishes his stone. He also was a tough taskmaster who insisted on perfection. Pity the poor assistant who let an unnecessary comma slip by or misspelled a word; J. A. Livingston did not suffer fools. Yet he could exude great charm, which was even more effective in contrast to his stern, brooding moods. I can still see him pacing back and forth in his private, glass-walled office as he sweated out his next column. Suddenly, as inspiration struck, he would rush to his typewriter and write his column at one sitting. Later on it would become my task to select a subject for the column, research it and write a draft. Once in a while my suggestions showed up in a veiled reference. That made my day.

Within two years the *Bulletin* was publishing my own weekly articles about Philadelphia companies, under the by-line Daniel Aaron, in the financial section of the Sunday edition. The first time my very own article appeared in print I was so excited that I traveled all the way to Times Square in New York City just to buy a *Bulletin*. To me, Times Square was the crossroads of the journalistic world, a Mecca for newspapers published in the United States. It was worth the ninety-mile trip to see my name in print at this shrine.

While I was worrying about what I was going to report on the next Sunday, my dear wife was expanding in size. Gerrie had stopped working as a "hooky cop" in her seventh month of pregnancy, and Erika was born over the Memorial

Day weekend, May 30, 1953. Gerrie and I were thrilled to realize that through our love the Aaron/Stone line would continue, and Erika's birth provided a new dimension to our life together.

As Erika grew from baby to toddler and as Gerrie's size began increasing once again, we began to look for larger living quarters.

William Levitt, a novel and creative homebuilder, had designed and built an affordable community of homes north of Philadelphia that he named Levittown, a new concept in housing developments. Homes were advertised for $9,990 with a down payment of only a hundred dollars. Although it would mean a forty-minute commute to work, Gerrie and I took the plunge and became house owners, made possible once again with the financial help of my father-in-law, Ed Stone, and my good friend, Jimmy Sax. Kenny was born in January 1955, a newborn in our first house.

Soon after we moved into Levittown I was once again confronted by ugly prejudices. Many residents of this "model community" had fled the city to escape other racial and ethnic groups and to join a homogeneous, lily-white community. When the first black family, the Myers, bought a home in Levittown, a group of us visited our new neighbors to welcome them. We found that instead of being greeted with the usual niceties of cookies and cakes, the new arrivals were being threatened by an unruly, hateful crowd that had gathered about their house shouting, "Nigger go home." The local police stood by and watched. While Gerrie returned to our home and children, I spent the night with the Myers family trying to reassure them that the situation would improve and that they would be accepted. Unfortunately, the pressure was too much and they left Levittown shortly after the incident, but I will never forget the fear on their faces. I could empathize: It is a state of being that I knew only too well.

Once I had established myself as a financial writer, the Philadelphia public radio station, WFLN, asked me to do a weekly commentary on Sunday evenings. I had never been on radio before and had no training, nor did I have a voice for it.

In preparation for my first broadcast of "Business By-Lines" to be aired on February 6, 1954, I spent days practicing before a microphone and talking into a tape recorder. I listened carefully to the tape so that I could improve my presentation. The best reading I recorded on my final tape for broadcast over the air.

I then proceeded to invite all my family and friends to our house to hear Dan Aaron's first column aired. While our guests were assembling, I delivered the tape to WFLN in enough time to return home to be with my family and friends and hear this remarkable presentation. I got home just in time to hear myself say,

"Good evening. Are we in a recession?"

All went well, and family and friends seemed delighted to hear their husband, father, and friend talking over the radio. I ended with my usual, "Good evening."

Then, to my amazement and the amusement of my guests, the tape started again from the beginning. Apparently the technician who was supposed to monitor the broadcast had fallen asleep. I tried desperately to telephone the station, and when my urgent call finally got through, I was able to stop the nonsense before it was repeated for a third time.

This is the script of that first business column I gave to the WFLN listening public under the title "Business By-Lines," Daniel Aaron, Commentator. (No need to read it twice!)

Good evening. Are we in a recession?

At a news conference President Eisenhower was asked just that.

He was asked more.

Ray Scherer of the National Broadcasting Company said: Mr. President, it has been suggested that there is something unethical, almost un-American about using the word recession in connection with the present business condition. What would you say about that?

The President answered that he hadn't seen those words, at least, stated in that way. He said this is a free country; one could use words as one saw fit. We are going through a readjustment. Not everything is now at its peak, so he supposed we had receded from something.

Others—in recent weeks—have taken less kindly to what they like to call "gloomy forecasts of a recession or of a depression." Speaker of the House Joseph W. Martin Jr. told an audience of seven hundred at the Benjamin Franklin Hotel here that "left-wing eggheads are trying to yell the country into a depression." The implication was that if they yelled long enough and loud enough, they might succeed.

This is not isolated sentiment. It has gained support in business and government. It has been debated on the Senate floor.

Last week Senator Kilgore of West Virginia inserted into the *Congressional Record* a column by J. A. Livingston, financial editor of the *Bulletin,* who had written, "Surely if gloomy talk could cause a business break, we'd have had it long ago. Throughout the postwar period, talk of a recession has been persistent and recurrent. If the prophets of good business really felt secure about the outlook for this year, would they try to shut up the prophets of recession and resort to name-calling?"

Certainly the President and his economic advisors didn't hush-hush facts in the Economic Report to the Nation. Says the report, "Since the summer of '53 we have gone through a readjustment. . . . It is the job of government to make clear its ability to face dangers in our economy and to take steps necessary to deal with them."

After a detailed analysis of this readjustment the President's economists concluded, "Our economy is basically strong. The current readjustment seems likely to be brief and self-correcting." But they warned, "The situation must not be viewed with complacency."

The real trial for the administration's confidence will probably come in the automobile industry. Some economists would say that the political future of the Republican Party is being decided not in Washington but in Detroit. And there, by two men: Harlowe H. Curtice, President of General Motors, and Henry Ford II, President of the Ford Motor Company. Since the middle of 1953 the automobile industry has been caught in a production race between Ford and GM—Ford in a drive to put the Ford ahead of Chevy, and Chevy in an equally determined push to stay out front. Plymouth—in self-defense—had to join battle. There is nothing sinister about this. It is competition, classroom style.

As a result, 1953, which started out as a quiet 5,500,000-car year, ended up in a Big Three production scramble: Output passed 6,100,000. By the end of the year dealers were swamped with cars. In the automobile industry the retailer doesn't give orders, he takes them. The dealer operates under franchise. He agrees to sell a given percentage of the company's output. Should he fall behind he would jeopardize his privilege to sell.

So when the Big Three poured cars into the dealers' showrooms, dealers had to find customers. They did, by offering big discounts. And stole sales from 1954. That is one theory.

Recently I had the pleasure and good fortune to meet Henry Ford II. He was good enough to answer some questions for this program.

(Getting to see Mr. Ford for this interview had been no easy task. Henry Ford had been warned by "his people" not to talk to reporters. He had sequestered himself in his room, and when he did venture to the lobby of the hotel he did so surreptitiously by the service elevator. I saw him enter the elevator on his way back upstairs and joined him. Before he exited, I asked him for an interview, which he granted:)

"Mr. Ford, it was been suggested that in your production race with Chevrolet last year you may actually have done a disservice to our country. Dealers in a frantic rush to clear floors sold cars at discounts, thus stealing sales from 1954. Do you agree?"

Mr. Ford answered for three minutes and then went on to say that Ford factories are working nine and one half-hours a day, six days a week, and would keep up that pace through May. Then production could drop by as much as 20 percent before workers could actually be laid off. Current overtime would absorb the slack.

That was two weeks ago and already Ford production schedules have been revised: sixteen plants are now on eight-hour shifts, and in some plants Saturday work has been eliminated.

Chevrolet, too, has pared production. It looks as if the auto industry will make 1,490,000 cars this quarter, 12 percent less than the record it had set for itself.

Maybe Detroit can absorb that kind of shock. But can the rest of the country? About 20 percent of the nation's steel goes into automobiles. Even now, the steel industry is operating at under 75 percent of capacity. It hasn't passed 80 percent since early December. The Great Lakes Steel Company, which supplies about 40 percent of the auto industry's cold-rolled steel, is laying off 2,000 of its 10,000 workers. Walter Ruether, President of the United Auto Workers of America and also of the parent C.I.O., says that since the spring of last year 74,400 workers have been laid off at Chrysler, Hudson, Nash, Packard and Studebaker.

The nation's unemployment in December was 500,000. Over 2,000,000 workers are now idle.

All this suggests that neither the automobile industry nor its suppliers—steel, glass, upholstery or rubber—can take a 10 percent production cut in stride.

In spite of this, the administration has put its chips on prosperity in 1954. If business doesn't take up the current slack, if unemployment should spiral, then the administration is ready to step in with public works, agriculture supports, and modification of the tax structure. Even now, the advisors want unemployment compensation liberalized, Social Security coverage widened, and tax laws changed so that, in the President Eisenhower's words, "Government will help build a floor over the pit of personal disaster."

Wall Street has cheered the President's confidence. Investors have bid stock prices to a postwar high. It is the investor's way of saying, or hoping, that readjustment will soon run its course, and production and employment will be on the way up again.

It would be nice to take Wall Street's word for it. But the only thing of which we are certain is that the future is uncertain and unpredictable.

I know that even President Eisenhower's economic advisors, though optimistic, have their fingers crossed.

Good evening!

At the *Bulletin,* Joe Livingston became my mentor. Not only did he give me a postgraduate course in journalism, but he taught me his basic rules for approaching a story:

1. Check your facts.
2. Write clearly and concisely.
3. Never be intimidated by power.

On one assignment I was sent to the Benjamin Franklin Hotel in Philadelphia to report on the annual meeting of a well-known corporate raider who was based in New York City. He purposely held the meeting in Philadelphia, far from the glare of the New York financial publications. To further guard his clandestine activities he forbade reporters to attend the meeting. Joe Livingston thought this was outrageous, and told me to get the story, period!

I got to the hotel well before the meeting, but I had no idea how I was going to obtain my scoop. However, on examining the meeting room I noticed a large heating duct on the wall next to the speaker's podium. Further investigation revealed that the duct also heated the room directly above the one in which the secretive meeting was to be held. Borrowing a ladder and placing my ear close to the heating duct in the empty room above, I found that I could hear all that went on in the "forbidden" meeting room. Presto! I got my story, and the article was featured in that evening's *Bulletin*. The scoop was not earthshaking but it reinforced for me Joe Livingston's lesson that "can't" was not an option.

By 1955, I had been with Joe Livingston and the *Bulletin* for four years, and I was beginning to run out of stories about Philadelphia companies for my Sunday column. I found myself spending more and more time in front of the

Teletype, hoping that something would move across the wires that would inspire me.

In early March of 1955, one ticker segment caught my eye. It reported an election in Dubuque, Iowa, where a franchise for cable television had been awarded to the Jerrold Electronics Corp.

What was the Jerrold Electronics Corp. of Philadelphia?

What was cable television?

9 *The new kid on the block*

I wasted no time calling Jerrold Electronics Corporation to speak to its president, Milton J. Shapp. When he came on the line, I introduced myself as a financial reporter for the *Bulletin* and asked for an appointment. (What a difference it made to speak to the president of a company as a reporter from the *Bulletin* rather than as a job seeker.)

Jerrold's production facilities were in South Philadelphia, with a business office located at Twenty-third and Walnut Streets. Shapp began our interview by telling me how his company had recently won the franchise to wire the city of Dubuque, Iowa, with what he called a Community Antenna Television System, or CATV. Jerrold had already designed and installed a number of CATV systems in the valley towns of Pennsylvania, where mountainous terrain blocked television reception from Philadelphia stations. Shapp spoke with a quiet, subdued intensity. He was clearly a man of great self-confidence and self-assurance, and he was totally absorbed in his new business venture.

Even though his systems were in the developmental stage,

"A man who couldn't be stopped" — Milton J. Shapp, pictured in the Philadelphia Evening Bulletin's *first news story about Jerrold Electronics and its entry into the cable-TV business, March 13, 1955. Shapp later served two terms as governor of Pennsylvania.*

Shapp predicted that CATV would revolutionize TV in America with systems that could carry twenty or thirty television channels, compared with the current limit of five. He foresaw that CATV would cover the American hinterlands as well as it covered the most populous cities and their suburbs, and would provide not only improved reception but also movies, sporting events and educational programs.

He then turned to his desk and picked up a piece of coaxial cable. (Coaxial cable is an inner core of copper wire surrounded by a layer of insulation and an outer sheath of woven copper or aluminum, all wrapped in plastic. Because the various layers of cable have the same axis, the cable is called coaxial cable.[10]) Holding the piece of cable in his hand, Shapp proclaimed, "With the use of this coaxial cable, television reception in small-town America will be as good as the television picture in New York."

Sensing that I was taken by his enthusiasm, Shapp insisted I meet his executive staff. I was impressed. They seemed bright, articulate, and informal. They shared their boss's enthusiasm for CATV as well as his sense of humor. This group was much different from their stiff, buttoned-down peers in the many companies I had seen. One employee whom I particularly remember was Barbara Lummis, a key executive who had been crippled by polio. I thought, "The president of this company has placed a physically handicapped woman in an executive position, and he has made it work." (This was long before the passage of anti-discrimination legislation.) Quite a guy, this Shapp!

Hurrying back to the *Bulletin,* I wrote a story that appeared in the financial section the following Sunday, March 13, 1955. It was the first time that CATV became a category on file in the *Bulletin's* morgue. Here's an excerpt:

TV ANTENNA WINS DUBUQUE IOWA ELECTION
By Daniel Aaron of the *Bulletin* Staff

Milton Jerrold Shapp, president of Jerrold Electronics Corporation, recently managed an election campaign in Dubuque, Iowa. The winner by 5,000 votes was his candidate: a TV antenna.

In a near-record vote, Dubuquers approved Shapp's community TV system and turned down a hometown applicant, the Dubuque Community TV Cable Company.

Here is what happened:

Dubuque, cradled among seven hills, was cut off from television waves. Even towering rooftop antennas costing nearly $300.00 each picked up only a faint picture.

The solution was a community antenna system. An antenna tower atop the highest mountain would pick up signals and amplify them. Then a coaxial cable would bring the picture down the mountain into town. Subscribers' sets would be hooked onto the cable.

Shapp, the original applicant to build the system, took his case to the voters after Dubuque's City Council, favoring a local firm, denied a franchise to his company. Although a report by independent experts, picked by the council, had endorsed the Jerrold system, the council was more impressed by the Dubuque firm's argument: "Send the foreigners back to Philadelphia."

But winning "losing" battles is nothing new for Shapp, who gave his firm his middle name because "it has been in the middle—and so have I—most of the time." Once again Shapp's knowledge proved persuasive and he won the franchise.

Shapp phoned to compliment me after reading the article. I thanked him for his call and told him, "If you ever need someone with my background, I would be very interested in talking to you."

Three-quarters of a year would pass before I received his call. The interim gave me an opportunity to look into this "new kid on the block," Community Antenna Television Systems. I soon began to learn a little about the industry's beginnings and the part Milton Shapp played in it.

One of the New Deal alphabet soup of agencies created by Congress in 1934 was the Federal Communication Commission, or F.C.C. It was charged with establishing a nationwide communications policy, with instructions to update these policies regularly and reasonably. Radio frequency allocation was one of the commission's first duties, to make certain radio stations throughout the country didn't conflict with one another's signals. By the 1940s, the very high-frequency (VHF) bands required by broadcast television needed to be allocated. This was the responsibility of the F.C.C., but the commission soon found that VHF signals were not as predictable as radio signals had been. Inherent problems with TV's black-and-white picture reception were further complicated by the advent of color TV.

In order to study these problems and ensure an orderly allocation of frequencies, the F.C.C. imposed a freeze on all new TV stations beginning in the fall of 1948. The F.C.C. assumed in its ignorance that the freeze would last only a year, but in fact it lasted four. The freeze halted construction of all new TV stations, forcing broadcasters and would-be broadcasters to sit on their hands until 1952. It was government at its most sluggish. The freeze meant that TV reception was limited only to those viewers fortunate enough to be in range of the hundred-plus TV stations that existed in 1948. Outlying communities were outraged because the F.C.C. had locked them out of TV reception that was available to their big city-neighbors.

With broadcast television at a standstill, the budding cable industry forged ahead. John Walson, who owned an appliance store in the small Pennsylvania town of Mahanoy City, had breathed life into the cable industry in the summer of 1948. He wanted to sell TV sets, but the reception was so poor that he had few buyers. Mahanoy City lay in a valley in the Appalachian Mountain range that blocked the TV signal from Philadelphia, ninety miles away. Walson discovered that although TV signals couldn't pass through the mountain, they could be received on top of it. So he installed an antenna on top of a telephone pole on one of the mountain ridges. From this perch he ran two army-surplus twin-lead wires down to his store. The results were remarkable

—a clear picture from Philadelphia and soaring sales of TV sets in Mahanoy City. Walson then proceeded to improve the signal by running coaxial cable from his store to the antenna site, or "head end." When he wired his TV customers to the "head end," he created the first Community Antenna TV System in the United States. That's the Pennsylvania side of the story.

By mid-1948 John Walson's neighbor, Aaron Liachowicz —appropriately enough, an optometrist—became the first of the more than seven hundred residents who brought their TV pictures into focus by subscribing to CATV.

Walson's next problem was those customers who lived a greater distance from his store, because the TV signal weakened as it became further from the source. Walson found that it worked very much like a water system. In later years, when I appeared before city councils for franchise applications, I would inevitably use this analogy: If a spigot is turned on far from the water source, the water pressure decreases with distance. To alleviate the problem, pumping stations are placed along the water line to bring the water pressure back up. The same problem exists when a television signal goes through a cable, and Walson found that electronic amplifiers placed along the cable would boost the signal to the proper level.

In 1948, Milton Shapp, then a 42-year-old sales rep for a group of electronics manufacturers, met a group of engineers who had invented a "booster" that could improve the reception of TV sets. Wanting to include this new device in his sales portfolio, he looked for a manufacturer. When none appeared, Shapp decided to build and sell an amplifier himself. With $500 and two employees, Milton Jerrold Shapp established Jerrold Electronics Corp.

In the late 1940s, sales of TV sets became a significant item for appliance departments in department stores across America. TV sets attracted retail traffic who came first to watch television. But each TV required its own antenna to receive the signal. A customer interested in a particular model of TV would have to wait until a salesman hooked it up to an antenna. By the same token, apartment dwellers needed individual antennas to view their own TV sets, and a forest of antennas sprouted on apartment house roofs.

Jerrold Electronics came to the rescue, developing a new system with one master TV antenna (MATV). Shapp's secret: coaxial cable and signal boosters, or amplifiers, capable of carrying multiple signals at one time. This new system replaced antenna forests with a single master antenna for each apartment house. It also solved the department store's dilemma. Shapp loved to tell a story about Sears Roebuck that I printed in my March 13 article under the subheading:

SOLD TO DEPARTMENT STORES

When Shapp, an electronics engineer, developed a plug-in antenna system for demonstrator TV sets in department stores in 1949, he had to beat down the argument, "If established companies can't do it, who do you think you are?"

Shapp would install his system at no cost until it worked, then sold it to Lit Brothers, John Wanamaker, Strawbridge & Clothier, and Snellenburg's.

When Shapp went to Chicago that year to "open up" Sears Roebuck, he took along two master antennas. While Sears engineers were testing one of Jerrold's master antennas in a laboratory, Shapp persuaded the manager of a big Sears store to let him install the second antenna on a trial basis. The manager agreed to the installation; he was irked because he hadn't been able to receive a picture on his demonstrators and therefore couldn't sell sets.

Shapp and Henry Arbeiter, vice president and chief engineer of Jerrold, worked around the clock installing the system.

They had just turned on the first set and had received a clear picture when the phone rang. On the phone was Sears' research director, who told Shapp he had found at least 30 flaws in Jerrold's system. He said they'd have to be corrected before Shapp could start work.

Shapp knew that was a mistake; the system was already working.

Jerrold systems are now in most Sears stores.

Another creative appliance salesman, Robert Tarlton, read about Shapp's new invention and thought it was just what he needed to wire Lansford, Pennsylvania. Using Jerrold's commercially manufactured boosters and coaxial cable, Bob Tarlton wired his home town.

When Tarlton realized how many boosters he was buying, he thought that a trip to Philadelphia was in order to see if he could buy them directly from the factory. Jerrold sales manager, Bud Green, remembers saying, "Oh, sure, we'll sell you amplifiers."

On a subsequent trip to the factory to pick up more amplifiers, Bud asked Bob, "What are you doing with all those amplifiers?" Bob Tarlton told him about the Lansford system he was installing.

When Milton Shapp heard from his sales manager what Tarlton was doing, he arranged to see Tarlton on his own turf in Lansford. The meeting took place on the Thanksgiving weekend of 1950. Shapp was duly impressed and offered to manufacture amplifiers that would meet the specific needs of Tarlton's new cable system. By the following Monday morning, Jerrold's entire engineering staff was zeroed in on designing boosters specifically for Tarlton's use.

On December 22, 1950, an article in the *New York Times* reported, "The town of Lansford, which heretofore had been barred from television reception because it lies in a valley, is now receiving TV programs regularly after erecting what is believed to be the country's first 'community antenna.'" Evan Whilden, the mayor of Lansford, was quoted as saying that the signals received were "Just as good as you folks get up in New York," and he added, "Ultimately, the single aerial might serve 30,000 valley residents."[11]

The opening of the Lansford system drew residents by the hundreds into downtown Lansford. The event made the front page of the *Wall Street Journal* under the headline, "Christmas Comes to Lansford, Pennsylvania in July." The article told of Christmas-size crowds coming downtown to watch TV.

These headlines were not wasted on Milton Shapp. Instinctively, he recognized that his company had to be more than just an equipment supplier; he also had to build cable systems in signal-blocked towns in America. But money was a problem—it took a lot of cash to initiate a system.

Wall Street was still nervous about the new industry, but Shapp helped pry open Wall Street's vaults. He persuaded four venture capitalists—Van Alstyne Noel, J. H. Whitney, Fox Wells and Goldman Sachs—to invest $200,000 in the cable-television system under construction in my old stamping grounds, Williamsport, Pennsylvania. One key to opening the vaults of Wall Street was a fluke in the federal income tax law that allowed cable operators to depreciate, or write off, the cost of their equipment on their taxes over a limited number of years, typically three to five years. After that, operators were disallowed any tax break for additional equipment. However, if the system were sold, the new owner could begin his own three-to five-year cycle of depreciation. The law made it less profitable for cable operators to hold onto their investments after five years. Many would sell their systems, then use the proceeds to buy back into the industry.

With enough cash from Wall Street to begin cabling Williamsport, Milt Shapp called Bob Tarlton. The conversation went like this:

"Bob, I have a problem."

"What's that, Milt?"

"I just sold a system to a venture capital group in New York City, and I need someone who knows how to construct and adapt the system to the Williamsport area."

Tarlton didn't have to mull it over in his mind for long. The Lansford system was doing just fine; by January 1951, a hundred homes had been wired and forty new customers a week were being added. Tarlton signed on with Jerrold, moved to Philadelphia, and began the process of bringing cable to Williamsport, Pennsylvania.

The first challenge presented by Williamsport was its size. No one had ever attempted to wire a town with so many potential customers. Special coaxial cables had to be designed and manufactured; distances to the "head end" were measured in miles rather than hundreds of feet. But the greatest challenge of all was competition: Two local cable companies had announced plans to build there.

Jerrold made a key decision, one that would become a cardinal rule for all its future projects: Concentrate on building a system where the greatest density of homes is located. This usually meant middle-class, blue-collar, working neighborhoods. Then spread out from there into the rest of the community. The gamble paid off. The competition focused on wealthier areas, believing that the affluent would be the most likely candidates for cable TV. Their assumption was dead wrong and cost them the business. Jerrold was also right in assuming that upper-class neighborhoods had many other entertainment options that the middle-class did not have. And there was reverse snobbery: "I don't watch television, do you?"

Within two years, Williamsport had become the largest cable system in the country. In three years, the Williamsport system was sold for $1 million, to the surprise and satisfaction of its investors.

The F.C.C.'s freeze, which was a disaster for broadcasters, became a bonanza for the cable industry. Cable TV continued to grow despite common wisdom to the contrary. The broadcasters had paid little attention to the cable industry; they considered it a fad. They forgot that cable systems did not use publicly owned frequencies and were therefore not subject to federal regulations. TV viewers, starved for additional programming during the freeze, didn't care how the picture got into their sets. This resulted in a shift of viewership from traditional broadcasters to cable.

When the F.C.C.'s "study" ended, cable was on a roll, and its growth in the next four years was phenomenal. In 1952, when I started my career at the *Bulletin*, there were seventy cable systems in place with 14,000 subscribers; when I entered the cable domain in 1956, 450 systems were in existence, and 300,000 cable TV customers had signed on.

With the Williamsport cable system underway, Shapp and Tarlton began crisscrossing the country, preaching the gospel of cable and applying for franchises in communities devoid of good TV reception. Those were the days when a franchise could be had for the asking. It was the money to build the systems that was difficult to attract; investors were hard to find.

One community for which Milton Shapp did find an investor was Tupelo, Mississippi, Elvis Presley's hometown. The investor was Philadelphia's Warren "Pete" Musser, who would become the dean of Philadelphia's capital investment community.

Little did I realize what a significant role in my business career Elvis's hometown would play.

10 *Shake it, Milt, shake it!*

As a new publicly held corporation, Jerrold Electronics had to prepare its first annual report in 1956, and Milton Shapp was looking for a writer. He remembered me from the *Bulletin* and the story I had written about his company.

Shapp's assistant, Zal Garfield, asked me to join him and Shapp for a review of their personnel needs. They clearly needed a public relations person, and I was offered the job. After some negotiation, I accepted. My job description read "Financial writer and publicity spokesman."

I had laid out for myself what read like a good year's start:

1. I would identify and establish personal relationships with the key players in the television, motion picture and cable TV industries, and the financial community.
2. I would achieve national recognition for Jerrold as the leading company in the new industry of cable TV, both in the consumer and trade press.

Although I had never produced an annual report, I had

studied many to prepare my Sunday columns on Philadelphia companies. I soon learned that it takes a team of three to write an annual report: a psychiatrist to be a guide through a "mine field" of egos, a writer to compose the report, and a rabbi to say a prayer over the writer's prone body.

The interruptions were constant. Somehow the mates of the executives, who never saw the office during ordinary working hours, all appeared on the day that portraits for the annual report were to be taken. These were the typical conversations, said and unsaid.

Mate: "Why can't you do something more with his hair?"

(Unspoken: That's because he doesn't have any hair.)

Mate: "I don't like his smile."

(Unspoken: That's because he never smiles.)

And so it went. . . .

At the rate I was going, with these interruptions I would never meet the printer's deadline three weeks hence. So I started a custom that served me well for the thirty years of annual reports that I have written: I disappeared into the stacks of the University of Pennsylvania library and did not emerge until the report was finished. Those were the days before cellular phones, and there were still places to hide on this globe. Let it be said for the record that the report was delivered at midnight of the deadline, that we were complimented, and that we were singled out for national awards for the report's clarity, financial analysis, and artwork.

As for publicity spokesman, I was equally wet behind the ears, but I had an idea. My goal was to prepare an article about Jerrold and its president and have it published in one of the local magazines. I discovered that *Philadelphia* magazine, in order to increase profits, sold its front cover for $500. For that price the magazine would headline an inside article on its cover. I paid the fee out of my own pocket, and the headline and article appeared. So, shortly after I got my new job, I was able to show the president of the company that he was on the cover of *Philadelphia* magazine. He thought I was a *Wunderkind*.

During the time I worked directly with Milton Shapp, he was considered the high priest of the nascent cable television industry. He was a genius, and it was he who set the industry's direction. He was accepted as the spokesman and was responsible for many of the technical and operating procedures that the industry follows to this day.

Milton Shapp, I soon learned, needed no help with creative ideas. If anything, my job was to help him keep his enthusiasm in check. His creativity did not stop with his cable projects; he wrote a musical called "A Man Who Couldn't Be Stopped" (guess who)? His appearances at the annual Jerrold Christmas party were legendary; he would appear on stage playing the violin, stripped to his belly button, with a woman painted on his chest that would shimmy as he flexed his stomach muscles. His exuberance was contagious.

Another facet of Shapp's genius was his ability to attract dynamic young men with vision to join his company. When Vice President Henry Agard Wallace, in his bid for president on the Progressive Party ticket, saw the handwriting on the wall and returned to raising corn, it was Milton Shapp, also a former party member, who gave many of the young, creative political operatives working for Wallace a home at Jerrold. They transferred all their skills from politics to business, and they succeeded in creating a fascinating and profitable company.

As I became more enmeshed in the fabric of Jerrold Electronics, I was gratified to find that my boss and many of his staff shared my own liberal philosophy of life. Many a staff meeting would conclude with discussions concerning prejudice and other social ills of our times. These meetings were to become incubators of ideas for me as I forged my own thinking and ideology about business and the inequalities in our society. In later years I would find that the two— good business and equal opportunity for employees—could not only co-exist but could be part of a lucrative business plan.

Zal Garfield, Shapp's talented assistant, took me under his wing. He had been one of Henry Wallace's key organizers, and I was enchanted with his ability to electrify an audience. For months I watched Zal carefully as he delivered a speech, studying his articulation, his stance and his timing. Soon I was able to mirror his technique. In years to come, when audiences would congratulate me on my excellent presentation, I would give all the credit to Zal.

By the late 1950s, cable systems and TV stations had become fierce competitors for audiences. Both industries had prospered with the lifting of the 1948 freeze on broadcasting stations. But the broadcasting industry, in a kind of paranoia, was convinced that the upstart cable industry was not only stealing programming from the broadcasters and charging cable subscribers for it, but they also feared that the cable industry was siphoning off advertising dollars. Broadcasters insisted that the F.C.C. designate cable a "common carrier" and regulate it as such.

To better understand the unregulated cable television industry, about which it knew very little, the F.C.C. initiated a "rule-making procedure."

A series of questions submitted to witnesses invited

to appear at these hearings covered the subject of pay TV. Security against theft of programming was of great concern to the commissioners because illegal connections to the system could threaten the business of pay TV before it got started. Once the security code was violated, a distributor of pay TV programming had no way to recover his costs. Of the witnesses invited to these hearings, three leading companies—Skiatron, Telemeter and Zenith—proposed distribution of programming over the air in scrambled signals. Not a single question was asked about cable. Milton Shapp, always ready to defend the use of cable distribution as the preferred choice, decided to submit a written presentation, even though he was not invited to testify.

Night after night I worked with Milt to draft what became known at Jerrold as the "Blue Book." It proposed a system of monthly subscriptions to cable TV with the option of additional payments for extra programming. This system depended on the use of cable, which Shapp considered the only way to guarantee system security.

Milt was indefatigable once he started on a project, and these sessions lasted so long that I would come home at two or three in the morning. Eventually Gerrie started to become suspicious and asked me, "Where the hell have you been?" My answer was always the same: "Working with Milt on his impending presentation to Congress."

One night I again came home late and could do nothing more than flop into bed. I was dead tired; I had worked most of the night writing explanations of why the Jerrold methodology was better than any other. I had written, "Even though the customer pays for cable, it is well worth the extra cost: The viewer will receive better programming and a clearer picture."

In the middle of the night, Gerrie kicked me in my stomach. I heard her say, "Now I know where you have been these late nights."

"Where?" I asked, groggy and half-asleep.

"You whispered it in your sleep; you said, 'It's better to pay for it than get it for nothing.'"

(End of story.)

Shapp asked me to call a press conference to challenge the three proponents of scrambled signals to a test of their security, and promised that within twenty-four hours his engineers would break their code. The challenge received press coverage from coast to coast. I remember one headline in a California newspaper: "Young Philadelphia Engineer Challenges Security Of F.C.C.-Favored Scrambled Television System." Shapp waited for his challenge to be taken up, but there were no volunteers.

But Shapp was not finished. He asked me to make arrangements with six television stations for a debate on the future of television, at which he would defend cable. The first debate was to take place in New Orleans. Shapp arrived at the appointed hour with his parents, Mr. and Mrs. Shapiro, who went along for the ride since they had never been in New Orleans; his public relations aide, Dan Aaron; and one folding chair.

When no one appeared to oppose him, Shapp dramatically unfolded the chair. Then he addressed the empty chair. A picture of his debate with an empty chair created another stack of clippings. Mission accomplished: In one week we had established the name of Jerrold in the consumer and trade press, had shaken confidence in the security of scrambled TV signals, and had paved the way for future progress.

Toward the end of the 1950s, the Senate subcommittee

on communications, not to be outdone by the F.C.C., decided to hold "oversight hearings" on cable TV. The subcommittee was chaired by the stern, forbidding senator from Washington, Warren Magnuson. My boss, as the accepted industry spokesman, was asked to be one of the first witnesses.

In preparation for the hearings I created a large cardboard display with pushpins that pinpointed the location of each of the three hundred cable systems in operation. We took this monstrous display with us, nearly delaying our flight's departure while we tried to juggle the map into a seat, protect the delicately placed pins, and calm the annoyed stewardess. (This was the first time I had set foot on an airplane.) Once we landed in Washington, we had a devil of a time finding a taxi large enough for my display and the two of us, and we arrived at the hearing half an hour late. As we entered the conference room, we inadvertently brushed against the doorjamb and were aghast to see all three hundred pins pop out of the display and scatter on the floor. Without missing a beat, Milton Shapp and I got down on our knees to pick up the pins and scrambled to restore all three hundred "cable systems" to their rightful places. Senator Magnuson pounded his gavel and asked the witnesses to please sit down. Shapp did so, but only after he had replaced the appropriate pins in the senator's home state. Out of the corner of my eye I noticed a slight smile breaking over the impassive senator's face.

Among the smiling witnesses sat Al Warren, the cigar-chomping, curmudgeonly dean of communications trade reporters. He was editor and publisher of *TV Digest,* the trade journal. The TV "fact book" he founded was the communications industry's Bible of statistical and operating information, with coverage maps for every TV station in the

United States. The coverage maps were like a pirate's treasure maps, because for those trained to read them, these maps identified areas of inadequate TV coverage, and were therefore rich potential for cable TV.

Al, whom I'd met before, came by and said, "Hey kid, you want to learn about the Washington trade press? Let's have lunch together and we'll charge it to Uncle Miltie."

Al was one of the few Washington journalists who recognized the potential of cable television and gave it fair and regular coverage in his *TV Digest*. His scoop on the Washington scene was the beginning of my education on the cable industry's place in the Washington power structure. Al and I became good friends, and we expanded our friendship to include our wives, Peg and Gerrie. Though our paths have parted, I will always be grateful for Al's interest in my career.

The session with Senator Magnuson was the start of Congress's education in the new medium of cable TV. Unfortunately, members of Congress were poor students who misread the cable industry for years, torn between the public interest and the powerful lobbying efforts of the broadcast industry.

In 1958, Gerrie and I had four children under six years old and we knew that there was no way we could stay in our small Levittown house. We began looking in the suburbs of Philadelphia and we found a five-bedroom Dutch colonial house on Marion Road in Elkins Park, where we would spend the next thirty years. Around the corner from our house was Shoemaker Elementary School, where our first-born blazed the educational trail for her sisters and brothers.

The scene of Erika's first day in kindergarten is duplicated a thousand-fold throughout the nation, but for Gerrie it was a new experience in child rearing, one that she has never forgotten.

Pushing the baby carriage with one hand and with Erika hanging desperately to the other, Gerrie began her trek to school, with Kenny, Jimmy and Jud beside the carriage, protecting baby Alison. All went well until the moment of truth arrived and Erika would have to leave the family to enter the halls of learning. At that point both mother and child started crying, Erika's sobs reaching to a crescendo towards hysteria. One of the teachers grabbed Erika's free hand and a tug of war ensued until Erika wisely decided to let go of her mother's hand. The scene hardly improved as Erika was led away and Gerrie, still tearful, gathered her remaining flock and retreated to Marion Road. The boys reacted with eyes bulging, wondering what was happening. Once on familiar turf, Jimmy, the most athletic of our children, suddenly jumped out of the first-floor window and disappeared. After school, knowing that her daughter would be uncontrollable, Gerrie was amazed to find a skipping Erika who happily announced she had made three new friends in school.

In addition to having the school nearby, a half-mile walk though the local ball field brought me to the Reading Railroad station for the thirty-minute ride to my office in town. But, at first, I did not spend as much time in our new house as I had expected.

By the late 1950s, Shapp's acquisitions of cable systems had become so extensive that he needed someone to head the department. I was put in charge of the cable division, which built and operated company-owned systems. I knew that this would mean traveling regularly to Mississippi.

One of my first tasks was to rebuild the system in Tupelo. At the time the system had 1,700 subscribers. To receive TV signals, the rest of the population had to use their own roof-top antennas, which brought them only two channels, neither of which came in clearly. However, existing technology enabled the industry to construct and operate systems that provided five TV channels. Our system upgrade allowed for this.

In order to take full advantage of the system's capacity, we picked up two networks off the air from Memphis. The cable operator had to use his imagination to program the three other channels. We used one channel for minute-by-minute daily news by training a TV camera on an Associated Press ticker. The camera swung back and forth at a calculated speed that all but the illiterate could follow. This was a precursor to CNN. A second channel featured Bubba, a live goldfish who hypnotized viewers with background music timed to the rhythm of his smooth strokes. This was a precursor to MTV. Our third channel was devoted to instrumentation showing temperature, wind velocity and direction. This was a precursor to the Weather Channel.

We should have known then that TV has its own special mystique and that one can create an audience almost from thin air. We spent many sleepless nights in fear of not attracting a sufficiently large audience for our cable systems, but with our creative three new channels, it became an unnecessary concern. The Tupelo systems achieved the projections we promised our investors.

I soon learned that the success of our systems in Mississippi depended to a large degree on decisions made 2,000 miles away in the nation's capital, where a massive assemblage of special-interest groups was gathering support for the federal regulation of cable. The F.C.C., together with the broadcast, telephone and motion picture industries, was proposing to place cable under federal regulation and require each operator to obtain a license. In the cable industry this would have had the same effect as the Stamp Act—it would have triggered a revolution.

My personal introduction to the F.C.C. was through a meeting we had requested with one of the commissioners of the agency. Milton Shapp, Zal Garfield and I thought it necessary to determine to what federal regulations, if any, cable was subject. The commissioner whom we met seemed baffled by our questions and sent us downstairs to meet with a young staff member who "was not busy at the moment," Stratford Smith. A good-looking, well-spoken and likable young lawyer, Smith knew very little about cable, but he saw the future in this community entertainment industry. He didn't have any answers to our questions at this time but he was making it his business to become the F.C.C.'s expert on cable TV. (Later, Smith left government and started his own law practice in Washington, where he used his knowledge to defend the cable industry against the constantly changing rules and regulations that spewed out of Washington. Eventually he was hired as the first president of the National Cable Television Association, N.C.T.A., while serving as Shapp's attorney to protect Jerrold's interests.)

Throughout 1959, Senator John Pastore (D-R.I.), head of the Senate Commerce Committee, held hearings on a variety of legislative proposals to regulate the cable industry.

The cable industry was divided into two bitterly opposed camps, the small cable operator vs. the MSO (Multi-System Operator). Small cable operators had standing in their communities and were therefore willing to trust their fate to local regulations. An MSO was considered a foreigner to the community, and his political power rested in Washington. The MSOs therefore preferred federal regulation.

In late 1959, after weeks of negotiation, Stratford Smith, by then the president of the National Cable Television Association, submitted what he considered an acceptable compromise. The board of the N.C.T.A., though split, agreed to support this version. The board's reasoning: It would be better to be regulated by the F.C.C., a federal agency, than a multitude of state legislators and local municipalities. Milton Shapp backed the Smith compromise.

That's when Henry Griffing entered the fray. Griffing was an Oklahoma Brahmin who owned Video Independent Theaters, a successful chain of indoor and outdoor theaters throughout the Southwest. With his chiseled features and his erect carriage, he stood above the crowd. Griffing had a lot of political clout, and his presence dominated any situation. He didn't command, he requested; and his requests were seldom ignored.

Griffing persuaded Shapp that federal regulation, once accepted, would become an epidemic whose spread could not be contained, and that instead of accepting the bill, Shapp must fight to defeat it.

Griffing knew that this represented a complete reversal of commitments made by the cable representatives under board direction; but so convincing were his arguments that Shapp galvanized his staff in a joint effort to defeat the bill. Milton put me to work: I was directed to send telegrams to all N.C.T.A. members urging them to come to Washington to join an industry-wide effort to defeat the Pastore bill. In response, cable operators from all over the nation descended on Washington.

I prepared and distributed to all senators and all attending cable operators a position paper describing the issues. We set up a headquarters in the office of a friendly senator where we kept track of visits by cable operators to the senatorial office. We posted a large chart indicating all N.C.T.A. participants and whom they saw along with what additional information was requested. Those of us who were more conversant with the issues accompanied the constituent operators. We conjectured as to how each senator would vote and charted our guesses. However, we did forget one item, which showed our inexperience in lobbying: We did not include a map of the Senate office building showing where the senators' offices were located. As a result, the long corridors were clogged with cable operators trying to find their way to their senators' offices. It was complete mayhem, but perhaps the confusion convinced the senators that these were truly local constituents.

Through our combined efforts, the hometown folks won by one vote, and the Pastore bill was sent back to committee to die. Senator Pastore was livid, and would never forget how the cable community had betrayed him.

No legislation against the cable industry would be enacted until 1968—and it would take a ruling from the Supreme Court.

11 *The best-laid plans*

In 1961, Milton Shapp announced his intention to run for governor of Pennsylvania. He called me into his office, told me of his dream, and offered me a key position in his campaign staff. Although I was complimented and tempted, I knew that my professional career would be better served working on my own, not in someone else's shadow. The company would not be the same, and it was time for me to move on.

But my departure from the company would be delayed by a year. Much of that year I would spend in Bartlesville, Oklahoma, the home of the Union Oil Company, working on the installation of one of the first pay-TV systems in the United States.

The project was the joint effort of Jerrold and the politically powerful Henry Griffing, who had led the charge to defeat the Pastore bill to regulate cable TV. He and Milt Shapp built and jointly owned a pay cable system located in Bartlesville. Griffing had chosen Bartlesville because it was within the coverage area of three Tulsa network stations.

If a cable system could make it there, it could make it anywhere, and he would be the first to know. With that knowledge he would apply for cable franchises in all major markets. Unlike many other movie theater owners who fought cable TV as a fearsome competitor, Griffing believed that cable would create a new source of revenue for the motion-picture industry. He saw the day when large theater chains would vie for ownership of cable systems.

On the Bartlesville system, newly released, uncut motion pictures would be offered on one channel for a monthly fee of $9.50. Pay per view it wasn't! But it would give some indication of public reaction to movies on television for an extra monthly charge.

Henry and Milton asked me to run the project. It was against my better judgment, and I told them so. I thought the project premature, and the mix of services confusing. I urged them to wait until Jerrold had successfully developed its Jerrold Cable Theater, which would provide movies of the consumer's choice and charge only for those selections. My caution was to no avail.

The Bartlesville pay-TV system opened with the exhibition of *The Pajama Game,* which had just been released to theaters. I can still see the headlines on our news release: "THE RESIDENTS OF BARTLESVILLE STAYED HOME LAST NIGHT, TO GO TO THE MOVIES."

The Bartlesville system had a successful opening, attracting a home audience of approximately a thousand subscribers. Viewers saw the newly released *The Pajama Game,* starring Doris Day, on the television screen rather than the theater screen. Unfortunately, the system did not retain its customers, and was down to three hundred subscribers when we closed it down to await another day.

I was convinced that pay TV would eventually dominate the television screen. Bartlesville proved premature, but not a failure; that's the message I carried to "Hollywood" when I accepted Henry Griffing's invitation to join a luncheon in New York City with the heads of many of the major studios. It was my assignment to report on our experience in Bartlesville. I urged "Hollywood" not to make the same mistake they had made when the broadcast television industry was in its infancy and they had turned down an invitation by the three TV networks to join them. By the time they realized their error and asked to join the networks, positions were frozen and it was too late.

This young kid from Philadelphia couldn't persuade "Hollywood," but he did convince the heads of a number of theater chains to invest in cable television.

As part of Jerrold's strategy we sought maximum exposure in the motion-picture industry, urging theater owners to obtain cable franchises in communities served by their theaters. Our goals were twofold: To bring business to Jerrold and to gain powerful allies in our fight to head off federal regulation of cable TV. We often took a booth at their national conventions.

It was as an exhibitor at the Theater Owners of America convention in Miami that I learned the value of having monkeys as marketing staff. Our portable exhibit consisted of a crude frame made of pipes and draped with a cloth, emblazoned with the slogan "Jerrold Cable Theater." It drew little attention among the giant exhibitors such as Coca-Cola, Pepsi and the leading producers of new movies. As I wondered how I could attract the attention of the crowd to our miserly display, I noticed a nearby exhibit for outdoor heaters that drew a steady crowd of onlookers. What they were watching was a monkey whose chain was held by a nearly unclad model. Every time a prospect passed the exhibit, the monkey would do a somersault. I decided to upstage them. I rushed to an exhibit house and rented two monkeys and found two attractive women at the Americana Hotel. The "Jerrold Cable Theater" soon outdrew the surrounding exhibits. Barnum I am not, but I sure learned how to attract a crowd.

By 1962 Milton Shapp had combined his office and factory and relocated to Fifteenth Street and Lehigh Avenue. I squeezed into the offices with Shapp, Zal Garfield, a secretary, and Claire Bloom, who later became the company's vice-president for cable operations.

The Bartlesville experiment had ended, and my responsibility at Jerrold had peaked. I was reaching a dead end. So I began to look for other ways to hop on the "CATV comet." Milton's able assistant, Zal Garfield, felt the same way, and in the fall of 1962 Zal and I joined forces to become brokers of cable television systems and franchises.

The decision to leave Shapp and Jerrold did not come easily. My son, Jimmy, who was only eight years old at the time, still remembers the nights I spent pacing the living room floor, trying to get a fix on what my plans for the future should be. At the age of thirty-six I was haunted by the fear that success was followed by eventual failure.

In the early 1960s, the brokerage business for TV cable was red-hot, and a broker could make a lot of money. All one needed to do was to find a buyer and a seller, hook them up, and collect a 5 percent commission. A not-too-uncommon transaction of $200,000 resulted in a $10,000 commission, a sizable sum in those days. At least, that is how it looked from the outside. Actually, I discovered that it took a lot of work to find buyers and sellers, and a great deal of travel to get a deal underway. If a sale did not succeed, expensive time had been wasted. I soon found the travel too demanding, and my time away from home began to affect my family life. Furthermore, I did not like the superficial relationships a broker established with both buyer and seller; there was always a sense of underlying suspicion that "the other guy" had gotten a better deal.

One of the early investors in the cable television industry was Warren ("Pete") Musser, who had made a substantial investment in Tupelo's cable system. Pete had decided to concentrate his limited assets on the development of a new company called Safeguard Scientific, Inc., and to sell the Tupelo system. Knowing of my experience in the cable business, he asked if I would help in selling the system. He needed a buyer; could I find one? At any other time it might have been easy to find a buyer for the Tupelo system, but the civil rights movement was in full swing, and liberal white northerners were less than welcome in the southern states. However, I agreed.

On a clear, cool, sunny afternoon, in the fall of 1962, Pete Musser and I found ourselves walking down Chestnut Street in Center City Philadelphia trying to figure out how to attract investors to the Mississippi cable system.

Suddenly Pete lit up, a boyish grin spread across his face and he said, "Here comes our 'fish.'"

"I don't understand," I replied.

"We are about to meet the man who is going to buy Tupelo," explained Pete.

Approaching us on the sidewalk was a good-looking, dark-haired young man wearing a Brooks Brothers raincoat; his name was Ralph Roberts. Pete and Ralph knew each other from the Young Presidents Organization (YPO). Ralph was flush with cash and ambition, having just sold his stake in the Pioneer Belt and Suspender Company (the same company once owned by Leo Heimerdinger, former president of the Foster Home for Hebrew Orphans).

We continued our stroll down Chestnut Street as a threesome, arm and arm, shoulder to shoulder, each "with a hand in the other's pocket." We learned that Ralph had sold his belt business to the Hickock Manufacturing Company, which then was the largest belt company in America. Although he had retained his men's toiletry business, Mark II, he was looking for a new business that would not be as competitive as the one he had just sold, one where he could be a key player.

"We've got the business for you," said Pete; "It's called cable television."

Ralph had heard of cable at a meeting of the YPO chapter, a meeting addressed by Milton Shapp. It sounded interesting to him; would I give him a crash course?

Subsequent meetings followed, and I began educating Ralph on the basics of cable television. The more we talked, the more evident it became to me that Ralph had decided to buy the business in Tupelo and had decided that I should come with it. As Ralph finally put it, "If I buy Tupelo, Dan Aaron comes with the sale and Dan Aaron runs the business."

The fish we had hooked was now trying to hook me.

"Why not come to my house in Elkins Park on Saturday," I suggested.

"Fine," agreed Ralph. "I'll bring my brother-in-law, Robert Fleisher, and we will talk."

When Ralph Roberts and Bob Fleisher came to our home on Marion Road in Elkins Park to invite me to join their venture into cable television—the acquisition of a CATV system in Tupelo, Mississippi—there was immediate simpatico among the three of us.

I had stored a small sailboat on a trailer in the back yard, and Bob was an expert sailor. We both had summer homes on Long Beach Island, off the coast of New Jersey, where we both spent many of our summers. Ralph admired a ten-foot antique dining room table that my wife had just acquired to seat our family of seven. Ralph needed a similarly large table for his family of seven. Having interests in common was a good beginning.

We sat down to talk, and in my own inimitable fashion, I began to list some of the problems we might be facing in Tupelo. For one thing, the systems manager, who preached the gospel over the radio on Sunday mornings, might not consider our coming to Tupelo as the Second Coming of the Lord.

The good news was that in an attempt to impress his former investors, the Sunday preacher had consistently understated the number of homes in Tupelo in order to claim 98 percent saturation. In other words, he claimed that more than nine out of every ten homes subscribed to the system. It would have been the highest saturation on record. Actually, the saturation was only 50 percent, which gave us an opportunity to add subscribers through promotions and direct selling and thus exceed our projections.

The bad news was that this high-tech system of five-channel capacity required a rebuild at the munificent sum of three thousand dollars per mile, money that this new venture did not have.

At this point Ralph retreated to our medicine cabinet to search for Tums to calm his churning stomach. Bob stepped outside to examine the seaworthiness of my sailboat. I figured that any two guys who, within ten minutes of meeting Dan Aaron, head for Tums or the nearest boat couldn't be all bad.

I agreed to join the venture.

My former partner, Zal, returned to college, earned his Ph.D. in psychology, and began a counseling practice in California. I had learned much from my friend Zal. As assistants to the president, "Zal Garfields" exist in every major company, even though their names might clutter the table of organization or not appear at all. It is the job of the "Zals" to make the tough decisions; it is the boss's job to learn from them and to help implement those decisions.

All that was left now was to get Pete Musser and Ralph Roberts to agree on the price of the Tupelo system, which, in retrospect, was not difficult. The almost insurmountable challenge was finding a time when these two men could meet; Pete stuck to the "early to bed and early to rise" routine, while Ralph's pattern was just the opposite. But I was determined, and we did get the two together to consummate the deal.

That chance encounter more than thirty years ago on Chestnut Street led to what has become a billion-dollar communications company, the third-largest cable company in the United States, serving more than eight million subscribers. It is one of the few companies among the Fortune 500 to have reached its present size in the lifetime of its founders.

Its name is Comcast.

12 *To dream . . . the impossible dream*

Early in 1963 I joined Ralph Roberts in his office in the old
Barclay Building, later called the GSB Building, on City Line
Avenue at Belmont in Bala Cynwyd, just outside Philadel-
phia. The eleventh-floor office was small, just one large room
divided into individual spaces by ancient, tall, metal file
cabinets. Five of us shared this space: Ralph; two secretaries,
Mrs. Ann Gardner and Kit Marshall; the bookkeeper, Millie
Zappacosta; and myself. Besides her secretarial duties, Mrs.
Gardner ran Ralph's flourishing toiletry business, Mark II
("The Mark of a Man"), contracting to have the product
made by a "filler" company in New York. Our quarters were
bursting at the seams, with no room to even think about
hiring another person, when along came Julian.

The powerful teen-ager who had played basketball at
the Neighborhood Center in South Philly had graduated
from high school with honors and finished his education
with a master's degree from Ralph Roberts's old alma mater,
the Wharton School of the University of Pennsylvania. After
graduation, Julian joined the Philadelphia accounting firm

of Adler, Faunce and Leonard and became a practicing C.P.A. In the late 1950s he spent much of his time in the outlying Pennsylvania communities with his firm's CATV clients. For tax advantages, he was helping each of these clients convert from a C corporation to the newly enacted S corporation. (Under the rules of a C corporation, all profits are taxed at the corporate tax rate, and then any proceeds distributed to the owners are taxed at the individual's rate, a so-called "double tax." In an S corporation, profits are allocated to the owners and taxed based on the owner's rate, thus avoiding the corporate tax on those profits.) While making these conversions, Julian learned much about the community antenna systems and reported back to his Philadelphia accounting office:

"CATV is the greatest business in the world. These guys put an antenna on the top of a hill, run wires through the trees to a central location, and then hook up individual homes to receive a clear television signal. They charge their clients $100 to hook up and then use the $100 to wire up the next street. There is a three buck-a-month service charge, they don't pay taxes, they keep it all; it's the greatest thing since stealing."[12]

After Ralph Roberts sold his Pioneer Belt Company, he called his local accounting firm, Adler, Faunce and Leonard, and asked them to assign one of their bright young accountants to work with him. The firm sent their young tax expert, Julian Brodsky. Ralph wasn't quite prepared for the accountant they selected. Julian was a powerful six-foot-two, with a dominating personality and a raucous voice. And he was ever so bright. Ralph was very satisfied with him and put him on retainer as the company's C.P.A.

Each quarter, Julian arrived at Ralph's office to do the

tax work for Ralph's toiletry business and for his small personal securities portfolio. It soon became evident that with Millie's help, Julian would be able to balance the books in a much shorter time than the allotted and chargeable eight hours. This allowed Julian to spend time chatting with Ralph, and this is how Julian became privy to the possibility of Ralph's new business venture in cable TV.

In early 1963, when Ralph decided to buy the Tupelo system from Pete Musser, Julian, who was fascinated by the potential of CATV, walked into Ralph's office during his scheduled quarterly visit and announced:

"You are not doing this without me. I have just resigned from Adler, Faunce and Leonard."

Although Julian had notified his employer of his intentions, it would be six months before he became a part of the organization. By the end of 1963, Julian arrived in our office with a card table and chair in tow.

"What's that for?" I asked.

"There's no furniture in here for me," Julian retorted.

So Julian and his card table and chair occupied the prime spot next to the door until we moved to larger quarters down the hall.

In the beginning, Julian wasn't terribly busy. We were operating only one cable system along with Ralph's after-shave business. So Julian focused all his genius, all his energy, all his financial training—which would eventually help our company raise billions of dollars—on dissecting my expense account. After days of Julian's torture about a luncheon at the local restaurant, Williamson's, I finally turned to Ralph for help, only to be have him show me the back of his hand to sample still another whiff of the newest and most calming scent of the toiletry business. (Scent is to the toiletry business what taste is to the winery; it takes a highly developed sense of smell. In those days, I would often arrive at home smelling as though I had spent the day in a bathhouse.)

When we purchased the Tupelo community antenna system, three other systems were included in the sale: Okolona CATV, just south of Tupelo on U.S. 45; West Point CATV, still further south on the same highway; and Laurel CATV, located close to Mississippi's southern border. A new ten-channel capacity plant was already under construction to replace the Laurel system. I took responsibility for supervising construction and operation of the system, and I soon learned every bump and turn on U.S. 45 as I traveled the two hundred miles between Tupelo and Laurel.

Through our travels in Mississippi, Ralph and I found Weidman's, the only restaurant in the state that served corned beef and coleslaw sandwiches and placed jars of peanut butter on their tables. Ralph was so addicted to their peanut butter that he would bring along his own large spoon in order to empty the jar before they took it away. Whenever they saw Ralph, they saw their profit for the day eaten up in peanut butter.

Once the new Laurel system was in operation, we found that a degradation of signal in the system was destroying the quality of the picture. The cable, which was designed to keep water out, did the reverse. It kept the water in, decimating the TV picture. The mayor of Laurel called me in Philadelphia and roared, "Fix the system or take the damn thing off our poles."

I could just see myself schlepping miles of cable on my back to keep the system running and to escape the wrath of our subscribers. The mayor didn't much care when I told him that the problem was common to all rebuilt cable systems.

I booked the next flight to Memphis, then drove to Laurel carrying with me a precious three-by-five package that I'd been given which supposedly contained the fix for our problem. When I opened the package in Laurel, surrounded by every employee on our staff, the magic ingredients turned out to be a dozen sawed-off broomstick handles with the instructions, "Beat the hell out of every inch of the cable."

It actually worked until the next rain, when the procedure needed to be repeated. Broomsticks became standard equipment on all our service trucks. Fortunately, a new type of coaxial cable soon became available that enabled us to replace the faulty cable and end this problem.

It was in supervising these Mississippi systems that I developed my theory of cable system management: The system manager is the center of our universe. He is the one who runs the system, takes responsibility for its performance and represents our company in the community. Our goal was to be a local company and not to be considered "foreigners" who pulled money out of the community. The only Philadelphia supervision was enforcement of the budget, which was shaped by the manager and myself in a series of tough negotiations. Once approved, the budget ruled *Britannia,* and these negotiated budget projections were used to borrow money.

I do not pretend to suggest that this approach is always successful. Some managers require more supervision, others less. I soon found that the Tupelo manager, whom we inherited, resented any supervision. He was difficult to work with and difficult to direct, but he intimidated me with exaggerated tales of his power in the community. It all fell into place in a conversation with a cabby on my way to the airport to take my weekend flight back to Philadelphia and my family. The cabby asked me what I was doing in Mississippi, and I told him we were rebuilding the local cable system. This prompted an stream of invective about the manager of our system. Was I aware the manager was a bigot and a whole lot of other things, too?

"Turn the taxi around and please take me back to the office," I told him.

I fired the manager on the spot.

This taught me a lesson I would not forget: People are basically the same all over the country. A person difficult in Tupelo is a person who will be difficult anywhere.

After hiring a new manager, I stayed on in Tupelo to determine how best to sell a product with which the potential user was not familiar. I soon settled on door-to-door selling. We needed something to get us in the door, but in those days we were short of money. Luckily, we found a Mississippi company that sold discontinued goods, and as an incentive to homeowners to sign up for cable, we gave away shoeshine kits. You could tell a cable subscriber by the shine of his shoes at church on Sunday.

Within a year we added Meridian, Mississippi to our portfolio. The story of how Meridian was brought on board has been the subject of company lore for years, and it goes something like this: "A young Ralph Roberts got into a craps game in the pine woods of Mississippi and wound up owning the cable franchise in Meridian, Mississippi." But the real story is just as wild and says something about Ralph Roberts's excellent sense of timing, once again being at the right place at the right time.

Meridian lies 175 miles from Tupelo, three-quarters of the way to Laurel. One day, Ralph was driving between the two cities on his customary inspection tour of the company's cable-TV systems. Late in the afternoon, he decided to stop at one of the local roadhouses for a little rest and relaxation. Mississippi in those days was "dry." Roadhouse clubs were set up to circumscribe the law; there, public drinking was legal, as was gambling. The clubs boasted that they had the best food in town, and I can testify that in most cases this was true.

Ralph stopped at the Queen of Hearts and, testing the laws of probability, found himself at the craps table. Ralph tends to talk with anybody who happens to be nearby; being the schmoozer he is, he soon began conversing with a young gentleman next to him who was also trying his hand at craps.

"You have a very interesting accent. Where are you from?" asked Ralph.

"Well, I am a Harvard graduate living in Meridian, and during my four years at Harvard I did my best to rid myself of my accent so I would not sound like I came from Mississippi. What do you do?"

Ralph told him he was in the cable TV business.

"That's interesting," Ralph's new acquaintance answered. "Today we had a referendum as to who would win the Meridian cable franchise. The contest was between Mr. Royal, who owns all the movie theaters in town, and Mr. Goodling, who controls the Dixie Trucking Company.

"Now I'll tell you something," continued the young man. "Mr. Royal is going to be very surprised, because he thinks he won. What Mr. Royal doesn't know is that a number of voter certificates came in late today, and after the final count, it was Mr. Goodling who won."

"How do you know so much about this?" Ralph asked.

"I counted the ballots. I'm the auditor for Meridian. And I'll tell you something else: If you go to the city council meeting tomorrow morning and watch them open up the ballot box, you can see for yourself that Mr. Goodling is the winner, and Mr. Royal is going to scream his head off. And as a matter of fact, if you want to buy the franchise, after the count go and see Mr. Goodling in his office. I don't think he really wants to build a cable system."

By this time Ralph had all he could do to contain himself. He let out a long "Ohhhh?"

Ralph spent the night in Meridian, and the next morning he appeared at the city council meeting. The young man was right: Mr. Royal lost the franchise to Mr. Goodling, and Mr. Royal did scream his head off.

After the proceedings, Ralph headed for Mr. Goodling's office to see what deal he could make. He found a huge office located in a "three-foot building." (The building extended into Meridian's commercial zone, which was in the next county, by three feet. This extension evidently gave the building's owner the lower tax rate of the next county.)

A take-charge secretary greeted Ralph and announced his presence to Ron Goodling. After congratulating the winner and making some small talk, Ralph said, "We are in the cable business. Are you interested in selling the Meridian franchise?"

The answer came quickly and it was to the point.

"Young man, everything I own is for sale, including them," Goodling said, pointing to a picture of his wife and two daughters.

A deal was consummated on the spot, and the Meridian TV franchise became ours.

In order to proceed with construction, a bond of $100,000 was required to protect the county from the possibility of our defaulting. Also, the franchise stated clearly that, within a year of the date of issuance, 90 percent of all applicants who desired cable must be connected to the system.

When Julian let the Maryland Casualty Company know we had obtained a franchise in Meridian, Mississippi, they issued the needed paper. But the local insurance broker for our bonding company was a good friend of Mr. Royal's, the sore loser, and he told our casualty company there was no way that we could fulfill the contract in the time allotted. He insisted we would forfeit the franchise, and warned that the subsequent legal fees would be excessive. It didn't take long for Maryland Casualty to cancel the bond.

We prided ourselves that whenever we entered a town where we wished to do business, we attached ourselves to the best people we could find. A senior lawyer of Meridian named Mr. Snow, a gentleman with flowing white hair and the look of William Jennings Bryan, was our contact. We took our problem to Mr. Snow. His telephone call to Maryland Casualty sounded like this:

"This is Mr. Snow of Meridian, Mississippi. I would like to talk with the vice-president handling bonding issues." When Mr. V.P. came on the line, Mr. Snow continued,

"I understand that your company cancelled a bond for Meridian Community Antenna System. I just want to tell you that if your company doesn't reissue that bond immediately, you will never do business in the state of Mississippi again. And if you think this is an idle threat, you tell your chief counsel what I just said."

Then, we all sat around Mr. Snow's office and waited. Sure enough, within forty-five minutes, a call came in from Maryland Casualty.

"OK boys, the bond has been restored," announced the man with the flowing white hair.

The sore loser still wouldn't give up, and at his urging, the city demanded a surety bond of $125,000 to secure Maryland Casualty's $100,000 bond. We phoned Julian to tell him that the money was due in twenty-four hours. In an amazing show of support, our Philadelphia legal counsel, under the direction of Fred Wolf of Wolf, Block, Schorr and Solis-Cohen, put up the cash, borrowing from the employee bonus fund.

Our triad was in full bloom. Ralph had purchased the franchise, Julian had arranged the financing, and it was now up to me to figure out a way to install the system in time to meet the deadline of the contract. The city of Meridian was so confident that we would forfeit that city council had already planned to allocate the $100,000 to purchase new voting machines.

In those days, all the players in this industry, including us, sold cable TV the same way: Once a franchise was received, areas with a density of seventy to a hundred houses per mile were wired. Less densely populated areas of a city might not receive service for months. The usual marketing approach was to buy ads in the local paper announcing a grand opening, rent a large hall, set up booths with TVs blaring, and sign up subscribers on the spot for cable service. We would almost automatically garner 20 percent of the potential users right away. For the remainder, it was a hard sell, using door-to-door salesmen and creative promotions. It usually took several years to reach the 50 percent saturation that was needed to make a system financially successful.

Meridian required a different approach. We could not hopscotch over the less densely populated parts of the community, because if we did, there would be no way to meet the required 90 percent service level. How could we possibly connect 90 percent of those who wanted cable?

After much soul-searching I decided: "Let's hide. Let them find us!"

We took offices on the top floor of the Dreyfus Building in downtown Meridian. We placed no identification on the door. The technical equipment we used was sequestered outside town; the trucks we rented had no signs; the drivers either couldn't speak English or were sworn to secrecy. We then used a marketing technique that was rifle-driven rather than the usual shotgun approach. Targeting the most densely populated areas we wished to cable, we started construction on a street-by-street basis. As we laid the cable, we mailed fliers to houses on those same streets, letting them know of cable's availability. Within a few days following the mailing, a salesman was at the door to sign up potential customers. The result: No one could sign up for cable until a salesman appeared at the door. We had 100 percent correlation of applicants to subscribers. And that's how we wired Meridian.

No sooner was the cable in place than a complaint was filed by one of the citizens. The Meridian contract had a clause requiring that the installation of cable would not affect the existing quality of the TV picture. The homeowner attested that before cable, his TV picture from New York had been excellent, but that once the cable lines were run in front of his home, his reception deteriorated and he could no longer receive New York. The accuser invited the judge to come to his home to satisfy himself that the New York station could not be received. It would have been national news had a TV signal from New York been seen more than a thousand miles away in Mississippi—so, as the accuser knew, the judge could not see New York on his TV screen. It was obviously a setup to keep us from meeting the conditions of the franchise.

I was called before the local judge, who granted my request for a thirty-day delay. This gave me time to fly in experts from all over the country to testify that the cable lines were not the culprit; reception from New York had never been available in Meridian. The complaint was dropped.

Not only did we comply with the terms of the bond, but we also received a glowing commendation from the city council of Meridian, congratulating us on a job well done. Stranger still, we set a record for the highest penetration of an original system, achieving nearly 50 percent immediate saturation. It occurred to me that selling door-to-door might be the way to market all our new cable systems. It made sense. We were introducing a new service to the community, and a salesmen at the door could explain the nature of the service and answer all of a resident's questions. Little did I realize that the industry would soon adopt my technique.

For our subscribers in Meridian, we published a newspaper bringing to them up-to-date news of cable. Included was a bingo card, and at noon every day we would televise the winning numbers. The prizes we gave away, such as a clock from the local jeweler, were solicited from retailers in town to avoid our being cited for gambling. Glenn Colvin, one of our installers and a native of Meridian, had a wonderful sense of humor, and he became our bingo announcer who gave the winning numbers over the air.

We didn't have many cameras in those days, and the ones we did have projected a very narrow visual field. Our whole studio was about as big as a card table. We focused the camera right on the numbers. Off screen, to add excitement to our bingo game, Glenn would imitate someone in our imaginary "studio audience." Using two voices, he sounded like this:

"Now here is a lady in the front seat. What did you say, ma'am?" And in a squeaky voice he would answer, "Oh, goody, you called my number!" Glenn later became manager of the Meridian system and then vice president and general manager of the region.

In another effort to interest the public in cable, we sponsored schoolchildren's trips to our "head end" antenna. We would then take pictures of the kids and broadcast them that night on cable, much to the amazement and delight of their parents.

Ralph was always interested in expanding our CATV business by purchasing more franchises, so when I enthusiastically suggested he think about Sarasota, Florida, he did. I had vacationed in the area, had seen Longboat Key and the other islands, and I was taken with the region's natural beauty and its potential as a vacationer's paradise. It was a retiree's dream come true. Seeing the sun go down over the island sands and disappear into the Gulf of Mexico didn't hurt. My intuition told me that Sarasota would expand and that this region held exciting potential.

The owner of the Sarasota franchise had done a poor job of promoting it. He had a wooden leg, and this prevented him from climbing telephone poles to attach cable wires. So, after obtaining a variance from the township, he laid his cable in the sand, just a few inches below the surface. In a hard rainstorm the cable became exposed and posed a nuisance. This didn't seem to bother the man with the wooden leg, who would simply recover the exposed wire with more sand. By 1966 he had a hundred customers with only ten or twelve miles wired. His company consisted of a large cardboard box where the records were stored, a bunch of ledger cards, and a beat-up old office on Pineapple Avenue with a tower on the roof that provided the signal for the "head end."

Ralph quickly learned that the citizens of Sarasota could receive CBS and NBC clearly even without the aid of coaxial cable. ABC's signal came from a greater distance than the other two network stations, but it could be seen clearly about half the time. As Julian put it, "In order to receive the networks, all the Sarasota citizens had to do was to hook a simple coat hanger to their TV sets, so why would they need cable?"

It had always been a cardinal rule that in order for cable to be profitable in a community, at least two of the three network signals had to be poor. Sarasota defied that principle. This did not bode well for buying the Sarasota franchise, but I was determined.

It was a hard sell, but Ralph finally decided to buy the franchise from "the man with the wooden leg," only to find that a few days before his call, Sarasota had been sold to a Texan for the paltry sum of $10,000. A call to the Texan revealed he would gladly sell for a profit. But the price was more money than we had.

Our contact at the Philadelphia National Bank, Jack McDowell, suggested we talk to Philadelphia's *Evening Bulletin*. For a stake in the business, Julian and Ralph got the *Bulletin* to put up the money. The *Bulletin* would own the system; we would run it. I started to rebuild the Sarasota system.

After the rebuild of Sarasota, we obtained franchises for some areas outside the city, including Longboat Key, and for the first time found ourselves competing with another cable operator who was franchised in the same areas. It became a frantic race to the finish.

We brought in a group of contractors and put Jerrold in charge of construction. We soon found ourselves meeting our competition head-on in the construction process. The final confrontation took place early on a Monday morning in a housing development.

All the utilities in the development were underground, and we were required to lay our cable the same way. We spent Sunday scouting for every construction vehicle we could find or rent. We needed machines that dug trenches and cut through bedrock, coupled with punching equipment to dig tunnels underneath homeowners' driveways.

That Monday morning, residents of the housing development saw the entire neighborhood in bedlam. We and our competitors were working frantically to claim as many customers as we could. Machines were digging everywhere. The punching machines needed to be completely immersed in a hole to do their job, and homeowners looked out their windows to see large holes next to their driveways. It took hours for the people of the neighborhood to find out what was going on.

By noon the mayor intervened and insisted we obtain permits from each homeowner to dig under their driveways. That brought an abrupt halt to the chaos. We spent the rest of the day in negotiations, dividing up the territory with our competitors.

A few years later, we bought out the competition.

Soon after, we applied for a franchise in Venice, Florida, twenty five-miles south of Sarasota, and won, beating out our competition, the General Telephone and Electric Corporation. However, our victory soon revealed a serious problem; a disgruntled GTE refused to allow us to attach our cable wires to its poles. What to do?

It has always been my belief that little is ever accomplished through litigation. Suing GTE for pole attachment was not the way to solve the problem. As a businessman I was convinced that nothing good happens when one goes to court. Julian and I were walking the attractive tree-lined streets of Venice when the idea hit me: "Hell, we'll bury the whole thing." So rather then string our cable from pole to pole, we buried it in the sandy soil (but unlike our predecessor in Sarasota, we dug deep enough to keep it buried in a rainstorm).

In the late 1960s the *Bulletin* became disenchanted with the Sarasota franchise. As Julian put it, "A guy named McLean, who ran the *Bulletin,* got out of bed one morning and decided that the world was coming to an end. He told his people, 'Sell off everything except my newspaper.'"

We desperately wanted to buy the Sarasota cable system from the *Bulletin,* but once again money was a problem. We had no choice but to help the *Bulletin* find a buyer. The Storer Broadcasting Company was looking for a property east of the Mississippi, and they offered the best price.

Julian, Ralph and I traveled to Storer's headquarters in the Midwest to finalize the sale. For the signing we met George Storer Sr. in his office, surrounded by memorabilia of his lifetime in broadcasting. I particularly remember looking at an old Zenith radio on his credenza as he recounted his entry into radio, when as an early advertiser, he recognized the power of this new advertising medium. I also remember the pained expression on Ralph's face as he signed away one of our prized cable-TV systems.

In subsequent years, when we applied for new franchises and the application asked, "Have you ever sold a cable system?" that same pained expression would reappear on Ralph's face. Camouflaged by a smile and through gritted teeth he would always give that singular answer, "Sarasota."

In a meeting after the transaction had been consummated, Ralph asked the eighty-year-old broadcaster if he realized that he was buying a cable system at an exorbitant price. He was paying three hundred dollars per subscriber, and it would take him ten years before he could get his money back. With all due respect, at his age and with this kind of projection, how could he justify buying the system?

Spoken in a deep southern accent, the words rolled slowly off George Storer's tongue:

"When my daddy started me in the communications business he was looking ahead for my future, and I am thinking years and years ahead for my sons. I am buying it for their future."

It was a lesson that the three of us never forgot.

As the meeting was breaking up, Ralph said to Storer, "Someday we'll be back to buy the Sarasota system."

Storer put his arm around Ralph and told him, "Young man, I have never sold a property in my life . . . and the company that bears my name never will."

George Storer was right: We would never repurchase the Sarasota system from the Storers. It would be decades before we would be able to buy back the Sarasota system, and when we did, it was part of a conglomerate owned by Kohlberg, Kravis & Roberts (KKR). The Storer children had long since sold out.

13 *"The boys"*

When we entered the CATV industry in 1963 in Tupelo, Mississippi, we purchased a six-year-old system that had only 2,300 subscribers. We rejuvenated that system and turned it into one of our most profitable cable operations, creating a blueprint for subsequent acquisitions. By the early 1970s, Tupelo was the hub of our regional systems complex, serving more than ten thousand subscribers.

In 1971 we acquired our largest system yet, the Westmoreland cable system, in the Appalachian Mountains of western Pennsylvania. It served 8,400 subscribers in fourteen municipalities thirty miles northeast of Pittsburgh, but in five years the previous owner had achieved only one-third saturation of the twenty-two thousand homes passed (wired to receive cable). Within a year we not only added fifty additional miles of wiring, but we were able to raise the saturation to 50 percent. One reason for our quick success was Sam Buffone, our system's manager.

We inherited Sam with the Westmoreland cable system. Unlike the manager of Tupelo I fired, Sam was the type of

"The boys" at Comcast in 1972: Ralph Roberts, Julian Brodsky, and Dan Aaron.

person who supported my theory that the manager is the center of the universe. He did his job, didn't need extensive supervision, and always had the company and his own employees at heart. He was a councilman in the community and was well known and liked. I have been particularly blessed by our lifetime friendship and the extension of that friendship to our two families.

Our company's headquarters were still located at Belmont Avenue on City Line, but we had acquired more space because we were growing, adding more franchises and more staff. As Julian put it, from our beginnings in 1963 until 1972, we were acquiring little "brother-sister" companies.

In those days we were a *gemuetlich* organization—easygoing and good-natured—with fewer than a hundred employees. It was not unusual to see even Ralph and Julian selling our services door-to-door. By 1972, the number of homes in our franchise areas numbered more than a hundred thousand, and subscribers to our cable systems were forty thousand plus. With the knowledge gained from ten years of experience in the cable industry, we knew that by stepping up our plant size, increasing our sales effort, obtaining new franchises, acquiring existing systems and programming creatively, we would increase our subscriber base.

In the early years, cable companies had to work hard to court bankers. Irving Kahn was the industry's cheerleader, twirling his baton as he applied for franchises from New York to Alabama. A man of boundless enthusiasm, he was loyal to friends, generous to associates, and a persuasive spokesman for the industry. Kahn had developed the Tele-PrompTer to display cues for actors and speakers, and he once told me how he obtained the bank loan for his first cable acquisition: While demonstrating his TelePrompTer to

David Rockefeller, who then headed the Chase Manhattan Bank, Kahn—with his legendary ebullience, I'm certain— told Rockefeller about the new cable industry. With a twinkle in his eye, Rockefeller responded by quoting his bank's popular advertising slogan: "You have a friend at Chase Manhattan." That's how history was made.

As our own company grew, so did our need for capital to finance our growth. We decided to go public. At the time the company consisted of three divisions: Cable Communications; the Music Network, which owned Muzak franchises; and Storecast Corporation of America, which offered a variety of in-store merchandising and manpower services for manufacturers and food brokers.

Four days before the initial public stock offering, we realized that we had to come up with another name; neither Cable Communications, Music Network nor Storecast Corporation projected the image that we wanted. For days we struggled with the name, and then, miraculously, we put together two concepts, *communications* and *broadcasting*. Surgically dissecting the two and then rejoining them, we settled on Comcast.

In June of 1972, 430,000 shares of stock were sold to the public, at $7.00 per share. It was our first public offering, with many more to follow. (A shareholder who paid seven thousand dollars for a thousand shares in 1972 would have seen that investment increase to more than $4.2 million by the beginning of the millennium.)

Three of us founded Comcast: Ralph Roberts, who provided the capital; Julian Brodsky, who guarded our assets; and I, who spent our assets in the construction and operation of cable systems. Actually, the delineation of our responsibilities was not so clearly drawn. We depended upon one another, sought each other's advice, and spent many hours talking through difficult situations. We also shared moments of emotional outbursts and cutting disagreements. But calming rough waters is one of the great skills of Ralph Roberts. We always ended by closing ranks.

Barbara Lukens, who became the company's vice president of franchise applications, recently recalled some of those meetings:

"Our quarters were small in those days, and when the 'boys' had their meetings, employees could hear their voices, especially when they disagreed with each other. I was appalled at the verbal infighting that would go on as they wrestled with some sticky problem. And then, incredibly, the meeting would break up and one of them would ask, 'So where are we going to have lunch today?'"

Hanging next to my desk was a cartoon that satirized the relationship of the three of us and our three very different personalities. It showed us at the controls of a racing car named Comcast: Julian pressed the gas pedal to the floor, I stood on the brakes, and Ralph had a firm grasp of the wheel. In the hallways and byways of Comcast we became known as "the boys."

Barry Diller, the Hollywood chameleon who reinvents himself with every new opportunity, describes Ralph as "the gentleman with the button-down collar and the stainless-steel stays." That's Ralph.

Ralph is a doodler, and his doodles are as revealing as the results of a Rohrshach test. Comcast was still in diapers in 1969 when I saw Ralph drawing what looked like boxes stacked one upon the other and spreading out in all directions in some indiscernible repetition. Ever more curious, I picked one of his pages out of the wastebasket and found it was headed, "Comcast Table of Organization for the year 2000."

One of Comcast's "ceremonials" was a meeting in Ralph's office. Anyone could call and suggest the roster of attendees; anyone could participate. Ralph would listen while doodling portraits of the attendees. After each executive had added his judgment, all eyes would turn to Ralph. He would stop doodling, turn to the group and say, "If it were my decision to make I would do such-and-such." Decision made. After all, he owned the candy store. Once, after the meeting, everyone filed out except Julian, who could be heard saying in a stage whisper that resounded throughout the floor, "That conclusion could have been reached by the two of us in two minutes."

One of Ralph's management concepts was *The Theory of The Roving Killer Trucks*. Whenever an executive was promoted or hired, Ralph's first question would be "Who'll take his place if he's hit by a truck?" Ralph believed in depth of management long before the company could afford it.

I remember a social gathering at which Comcast's culture became the subject of discussion. It was described as aggressive, determined, guided by a grand plan, moderated by compassion and concern, serious about its goals, but maintaining a sense of humor about itself. I noted it down because it was an amazing description of the personality of Ralph Roberts.

Ralph is the ultimate entrepreneur. His sense of timing is precocious. He mulls over his strategy endlessly, but once he goes into action, sparks fly. When he attains his goal he modestly withdraws and lets others take the credit. He has participated in every major decision of the company. That the company mirrors Ralph's personality is undoubtedly the greatest tribute we can pay him.

*Coming out on top — with the help of a chair — at a
party celebrating my retirement from Comcast in 1991,
with cardboard cutouts of my longtime partners,
Ralph Roberts and Julian Brodsky. (Photograph
© 1991 Howard Gordon.)*

Julian, on the other hand, does not bide his time behind
doodles. He's too feisty for that. He is a South Philadelphia
boy who grew into a Wall Street legend, raising billions of
dollars for a start-up company in a new industry, and who
survived by using his financial skills, his powerful memory,
and his absolute confidence in cable television. He has tested
every legal loophole so that the Comcast need pay no more

than its fair share of taxes. He has used every technique in the book to fuel the company's capital needs, including tapping foreign capital, limited partnerships and insurance company loans. These insurance loans permitted Comcast to pay only interest for the first ten years; after ten years, repayment of principal began. Under Julian's watchful eye we never missed a bank loan payment, our financial projections were right on the mark, and we were always cash-flow positive.

I had my own agenda for our company, which my associates shared with me: to build a company of integrity, and to be a leader in this new industry, a leader concerned for its people, where work could be a joy as well as a challenge. Then we could attract the best and the brightest, and we'd be on our way.

It worked.

From Ralph, I learned to reach for the stars.

From Julian, I learned how to turn dreams into reality.

From my associates at Comcast, I learned the meaning of friendship.

Comcast's cable division dominated the company, and the other two divisions, Music Network and Storecast Corporation of America, were profitably sold after years of operation. We began to focus exclusively on cable.

For the first few decades our game plan was to concentrate on those areas in the country that could not receive a clear signal from the three network channels. Since our first cable system acquisition, we had concentrated on more traditional CATV markets, those blocked by topography or distance from a full range of satisfactory television reception. We knew that these outlying markets would not be affected by what happened in the large urban markets. Our decision to stay out of the big cities and suburbs proved prudent.

Comcast was awarded franchises for the Philadelphia area in 1966, but following that award, the rules of the game changed. The imposition of rules and regulations by Congress and the F.C.C. made wiring the large cities impossible. Because of these restrictions another twenty years passed before we wired the city of Philadelphia.

In 1972, Ralph asked me if I would take charge of writing Comcast's annual reports. I felt a sense of déjà vu: Had not Milton Shapp asked me that same question sixteen years earlier? For the next twenty years I disappeared for weeks at a time, sequestered in the stacks of the University of Pennsylvania library to write our annual reports.

For the 1974 annual report, to show that we did not take ourselves too seriously, we called the humorist Art Buchwald and asked him to author the report. He thought about it for a minute and turned us down, saying he might want to rake Comcast over the coals sometime and didn't want to be hindered by any previous relationship. Then he added jokingly,

"Ask George Plimpton, author of *Paper Lion.* He'll do anything for money."

So Ralph and I went to see George Plimpton in his home on the Upper East Side of Manhattan. He had just published his first-person account of the sport of football, *Paper Lion.* Plimpton's shtick was to become a member of the institution about which he wrote; in the case of the *Paper Lion,* he had joined the summer training camp of the Detroit Lions as quarterback.

He laughed off Art Buchwald's comment and showed a serious interest in writing about cable, to which he subscribed. He agreed to write an article from the viewpoint of a cable subscriber, and what started out as a lark became a classic description of cable entertainment.

Under the heading "Easier To Follow Football on Cable Television," George Plimpton told our shareholders:

> It is easier to follow football on cable television than from a preferred position on the bench.
>
> I still recall the game that turned me into a paper lion: Detroit versus Cleveland. I found it difficult to follow the game from the bench. The players milling in the ruck of a play were difficult to spot against the multicolored background of the stands opposite, and the intricate patterns of their maneuvers were not apparent. Even the coaches standing up on the sidelines often seemed confused if the angle of their vision was difficult, and they'd call out,
>
> "What the devil was *that* play?"
>
> Not so on cable TV: Pictures are consistently clear, in focus, and in sharp contrast . . .
>
> For the Plimptons, watching cable television has become a family activity. For us, as for the millions of cable subscribers throughout the county, there's increased viewing—stations coming into sharp focus that were just a blizzard on the screen before with dimly perceived shapes and discombobulated voices . . .
>
> I would guess that just about everyone in a few years' time is going to be on the cable, even football coaches on the sidelines who, after they see the play clearly, may then shout,
>
> "*Why* the devil that play?"[13]

A recession tests the economic resiliency of a business enterprise. It forces management to re-examine assumptions which in years of economic expansion were accepted as truisms.

One commonly held belief in the cable-TV industry has been that cable is less subject to the effects of recession than are many other sectors of our economy. It is argued that families beset by financial anxieties turn to cable television as an inexpensive form of entertainment and escape. Comcast's experience in 1974 confirmed that assumption.

Despite a year of nationwide recession, Comcast's eight cable systems served 47,766 subscribers at year-end and had record revenues of more than $2.5 million, a 13 percent increase over the previous year. Even in Westmoreland County, Pennsylvania, whose residents were largely dependent on the local steel industry that was hard-hit by the recession, the number of subscribers actually increased.

However, the price of Comcast stock was far from recession-proof. By 1974, the issuing price of $7.00 two years earlier had bottomed to seventy-five cents, the cost of a glass of beer.

To satisfy our insatiable need for more capital, we turned to public offerings. A traditional Wall Street technique to introduce a public stock issue is the so-called road show or dog-and-pony show. Representatives of the lead underwriter and executives of the company go on the road to make presentations about the company for the underwriters, financial analysts and brokers who will handle the sale to the public to hear our presentation.

In the early days, when we shared those responsibilities, I would report on our cable operations, and Ralph and Julian made the presentation on the company. Rarely does the public attend these meetings. However, at one of these performances in Chicago, the underwriter bought newspaper ads and sent mailings inviting the public. A surprisingly large audience of some five hundred potential investors showed up. At the end of the presentation one member of the audience raised her hand and directed a question to Ralph:

"Mr. Roberts," she began. "I am a schoolteacher and I have my retirement funds invested in a diversified portfolio. I am so impressed by your presentation I would consider switching all my investments to Comcast. What do you think?"

"Don't you do it," said Ralph. "I would never invest all of my life savings in a single company, not even Comcast." Members of the audience nodded their heads in agreement.

Because of the nature of my work, I was often away from home. Although my responsibilities took me far beyond Philadelphia, I made it a rule to be home every weekend and to spend no more than three nights away at any given time. When going out of town I made arrangements not to leave the house until Monday morning. I wanted to help Gerrie in rearing our children, and I wanted to be there to see my five kids grow up. When I had to be away, Gerrie and I spoke on the phone every night.

By my own behavior I tried to set an example to the rest of the company as to how to balance responsibility to family and to the company. If an employee called a serious conflict to my attention, I always took the position that family responsibility came first. Whenever I traveled to a cable community, I held dinners for our employees and their mates. I made it a policy to recognize the contributions that employees and their mates made to the company's growth. I was keenly aware that a solid family life helped sustain a dedicated employee, and on several occasions I sponsored seminars on the subject of dual responsibility to family and company. At these seminars we recognized mates of the employees for their contributions to the company, whether that contribution was waiting up late at night while an employee made an emergency service call, or fulfilling a special request from the local mayor. I did not agree that the company always comes first.

When my coworkers questioned what they considered nonessential expenditures such as dinners for our workers and their mates, I would reply by quoting Time founder Henry Luce: "The profit motive, while useful, was not noble." Job satisfaction and the exercise of responsibility play an equally important role.

In my own job-conscious community of Elkins Park, my kids were asked repeatedly what their father did for a living. When they explained that their father provided distant television signals generally not available in the community, that it was called cable television and that there was a charge for the service, no one could understand. Living in the Philadelphia area, where free television reception was the norm, people could not understand why anyone would pay for such a service. Finally, my kids gave up and settled on the explanation, "My father is an antenna salesman."

In December of 1975, the RCA communications satellite SATCOM F-1 was launched into space. As the large white plumes from the Delta II engines disappeared into the stratosphere, few realized that the launch of SATCOM F-1 would revolutionize the cable industry. A new delivery system for broadcasting was now available. No longer was television shackled to the confines of Mother Earth and microwave transmission. By using satellite transducers and earth stations, orbiting satellites twenty-three thousand miles in outer space could transmit new programming to their viewers. Because of the cost savings of this advance in technology, pay-per-view would become commercially viable.

Within two years of SATCOM's entry into space we were building earth stations to receive the signals and introducing exciting new programs to our subscribers. In May of 1977, twenty thousand Comcast subscribers in the fifteen communities just west of Pittsburgh received an unusual announcement in their mail. They were invited to a free, five-night sneak preview of premium movies and special events, right in their living rooms. That's how we first introduced Home Box Office, the pay cable network owned by Time, Inc. to the Comcast system. After five days, more than three thousand subscribers had added HBO to their cable-TV service.

A single cost-effective earth station did the job of the old multi-hop, terrestrial microwave system. The link-up of satellite communications with cable-television systems created a new national television network almost overnight. In the next few years we equipped all of our systems with earth stations to take advantage of this cornucopia of new programming. It was just what I had predicted would happen when I analyzed the failure of the Bartlesville, Oklahoma, pay-per-view television system in 1961. I was convinced that pay cable would eventually dominate the television screen. Satellites were the answer, and a subscription system was the means. To the cable operators, this meant an added revenue stream.

Comcast was on the move. By 1977, five years after going public, we had doubled our number of subscribers to more than eighty thousand and increased our annual gross revenue to more than six million dollars. The company had grown out of diapers, passed through its childhood and entered its adolescence.

The year 1978 would be a busy one for me. In addition to my duties as Comcast's vice-president and as director and president of Comcast cable communications, I was asked by the board of the N.C.T.A. to serve as its chairman. With headquarters in Washington, D.C., the National Cable Television Association had been established to represent the industry to Congress and to regulatory agencies on the national, state and local levels.

The ubiquitous suitcase would be packed once again, but this time for two. I wasn't going without Gerrie.

14 *Mr. Chairman*

As the cable industry matured, and as it came under greater scrutiny by Congress and the F.C.C., Comcast became more active in the National Cable Television Association, the cable industry's lobbying voice in Washington. By the late 1960s, because of my growing experience in the ways of Washington, I was invited to become more active in the leadership of the N.C.T.A.

At that time, members of the N.C.T.A. board were elected by the membership-at-large and not, as they are today, appointed by the largest members. The board at that time was a club made up of cable's "good old boys." In 1973 I waged a campaign for a position on the board against a vice-president of Time-Life who was also seeking election. As a publicity stunt, I asked Ralph Roberts to go back to the same merchandiser who had supplied us with shoeshine kits in Meridian. This time I bought the supplier's stock of pocket tape measures. I had Sam Buffone distribute them to members-at-large as they entered their meetings, along with a leaflet entitled, "Dan Aaron. Take the measure of the man."

Sam reported that several members told him that the slate of candidates was pretty well filled.

But at five-foot-seven, I beat my six-foot opponent.

That was the last election in which I had to run. Two years later I became a member of N.C.T.A.'s executive board; then I was elected vice-chairman of the N.C.T.A. for 1976–1977, and became chairman for 1977–78.

My legacy to the National Cable Television Association was the hiring of Bob Schmidt as president, starting a leadership dynasty that passed from Schmidt to Tom Wheeler to Jim Mooney. Before 1975, the presidency had been a transitory job, an office occasionally vacant while the board looked for someone to fill the post.

Bob Schmidt had developed influence as a staff member of the Democratic National Committee. He became a protégé of former Ohio governor Michael V. DiSalle, whom he had met while a volunteer driver at the 1960 Democratic national convention. Bob had been a star quarterback at U.S.C. and had served for a decade as the public affairs V.P. of International Telephone and Telegraph Company. He knew his way around Washington, and he also understood some of the problems that the cable industry faced.

When I invited the N.C.T.A. board to meet with Bob Schmidt for a final interview, I extracted a promise that a divisive issue currently under discussion by the board, payment for copyrighted material, was not to be raised at the interview. To set the tone, Bob told of how he had become familiar with cable through his mother, who was a cable subscriber. One of the board members at the interview was a cable operator from West Virginia, Bill Turner, who was "hot under the collar" about the copyright issue: There was no way he would pay a fee to broadcast programs from other networks. Up went his hand. "Oh, oh," I thought. "Here it comes." Turner was a man of great determination who had just blown up his house while building a backyard swimming pool. With a slight smile, he said, "Mr. Schmidt, I am sworn not to ask how you feel about copyright payments. Let me ask instead, how does your poor old mother feel about having to pay a copyright fee?" That broke the tension of the meeting: Bob Schmidt was hired.

Within six months of taking over the N.C.T.A. presidency, Schmidt hired as his deputy Tom Wheeler, a savvy thirty-year-old from the trade association representing grocers, who would succeed him three years later. Schmidt was Mr. Outside; his handshake turned into a bear hug envied by many a politician. He looked like the star football player he had been at Southern Cal. Tom Wheeler was his handsome, enthusiastic, energetic counterpart. He was Mr. Inside, who revitalized a demoralized N.C.T.A. staff and helped turn N.C.T.A. into one of the most effective lobbying organizations in the country.

As Tom Wheeler remembers it, "1975–1979 was a time of incredible transition for the cable industry. The old community-antenna business was maturing into a national cable industry, and, as with any change, there was much trauma and turmoil. Two schools of thought prevailed in the industry. On one side were the independent operators who had pioneered the business. Their philosophy was, 'We started as a community-antenna system and that's the way it should remain. It has always been this way, don't change it.' On the other side were the folks who said that cable television was a larger, national commercial opportunity with greater horizons. They were the multiple systems operators (MSOs).

"For years the copyright owners, egged on by the broadcasters, insisted that the cable operators were not playing by the rules. They dubbed them 'pirates' who were stealing signals. Coming to a head in the late 1960s and 1970s, the copyright owners went to court and sued. Two separate Supreme Court decisions stated clearly that the cable operators had no obligation to pay copyright fees for the signals they picked up. The high court's decision legalized the cable operator's ability to import a signal from another TV market with no payment to the copyright owner.

"So infuriated by the decision of the Supreme Court were the broadcasters and the copyright owners that they persuaded the F.C.C. to act. Their logic: If the cable industry could import programs and not pay for them, the broadcasters who did pay for programming were going to make sure that they were not at a disadvantage.

"Responding to the considerable pressures of the broadcasters, the F.C.C. passed a series of restrictive rules. These rules limited the services the cable operators could sell, and thus limited the desirability and demand for their product.

"One very limiting rule restricted cable operators to importing only two distant signals. Just as damaging was the syndicated exclusivity requirement: If a local TV station was showing a syndicated program such as *M*A*S*H*, *Star Trek* or *Hogan's Heroes*, the cable operator was forbidden to show that same program on cable, even at a different time.

"It became obvious that if you wanted to see *Star Trek* you could only see it by tuning in to your local broadcaster. The cable operators were put into a position that told them they could deliver a couple of chunks of cheese—and, by the way, it's going to be Swiss cheese. The rules left the cable operators with little new to sell.

"Until the cable industry could get around those restrictions, they did not have the potential to expand into major markets or into a more pervasive medium. If this industry was to survive, the cable operators had to get on the other side of the copyright issue and, so doing, eliminate the rationale underpinning the rules. Enter Dan Aaron!

"What Dan Aaron was able to do, and the reason Dan was thrust into that leadership role during these times of angst, was because he was Dan Aaron. He was not a showboat; he was not, 'Oh, I am so great and I am impressed with myself.'

"Dan came out of the community-antenna environment and knew the cable business. He was a smooth, trustworthy, rational individual who could, as a result of those personality traits, become a conduit through which both parties could relate and talk. At the same time, Dan was a leader. In his own quiet, unassuming way, he moved things beyond the status quo. And he did it without ever being offensive or confronting those who held to the old ways. Dan kept the peace."[14]

At this point, Tom and some others of us recognized that growth for the cable industry meant having to step up to the plate and deal with the copyright issue. Equally strong was a group of cable pioneers who said, "Over our dead bodies! We will never pay a cent for copyright."

Because I had come out of the community-antenna environment and knew the business, I was asked to take a leadership role.

It took some time and some gentle persuasion, but eventually the cable operators sat down with the copyright owners and said, "OK, let's cut a deal." The concept was that cable operators would receive a compulsory license enabling them to carry network programs in return for paying a royalty administered by a government agency, the Copyright Royal Tribunal.

The logjam was broken, and the foundation was laid for the industry to seek repeal of the F.C.C.'s restrictive rules.

Another big problem facing the cable-TV industry during the late 1970s was a conflict with independent telephone companies. Cable operators, for the most part, used local utility poles to string their wires. The utility companies were demanding payment for the use of their poles, and in the early 1960s, the American Telephone and Telegraph Company had reached an agreement with the N.C.T.A. on a nationwide uniform rate policy for using AT&T poles. But the independent telephone companies had refused to sign on. By the mid-1970s, the independents had become increasingly restrictive by raising attachment fees and, in some cases, even demanding a piece of the action.

California was the first state to wrestle with the problem and pass a uniform pole-attachment bill. Subsequently, the cable industry sought relief from the F.C.C. After ruling that the F.C.C. had no authority to regulate the utilities, the F.C.C. turned the request over to Congress.

It was on my watch as the chairman of the N.C.T.A. that Representative Timothy Wirth (D-Colorado) sponsored a pole-attachment bill. Two days after I was elected chairman, in 1977, I appeared before a congressional committee to discuss the pole-attachment question. The hearing lasted all day and into the night.

Following tradition, members of the congressional committee received copies of the testimony that each witness then read. As I began my testimony, I noticed that the members were looking at the printed material but were not paying attention to what I was saying. I had prepared all day for my time before the committee and, as far as I was concerned, its members owed me the courtesy of listening to my testimony. I was determined to make them look at me and hear what I had to say. So I began to give testimony that differed from the printed page. The congressmen were not used to that, and were thoroughly confused. They kept leafing through the printed testimony, trying to find their place. Finally they gave up and gave me their undivided attention. I had won, and they let me finish my testimony. They also remembered me from then on.

One of my special interests was equal employment opportunity, the affirmative-action program. Years before I had made a commitment: If I were ever in a position to do so, I would be actively involved in employing minorities. N.C.T.A.'s new president, Bob Schmidt, shared my belief that our own national organization was a good place to start.

Bob Schmidt scoured the country for minority personnel. He found and hired Bob Johnson, an African American, to head the N.C.T.A.'s work on pay cable. After working with us for many years, Bob left to start KBLE, the first cable channel geared expressly to the interests of minorities, particularly African Americans. With this vision and the financial help of John Malone, a member of N.C.T.A. and a successful Denver cable operator, Bob launched Black Entertainment Television (BET). By the turn of the twenty-first century, Bob Johnson's channels—BET, BET On Jazz and Action Pay Per View—would be reaching more than fifty million subscribers around the world, and his BET holdings would be sold to Viacom for over two billion dollars.

In June of 1978, the Senate held hearings on the subject of equal opportunity. Senator Fritz Hollings echoed my commitment to equal employment opportunity. Tall and distinguished looking, a southern gentleman directly out of central casting, the liberal Democratic senator from South Carolina asked a question of his witness slowly and sincerely in his native southern drawl:

"Mr. Aaron, what is the cable industry doing to comply with the Equal Employment Opportunity Act?"

I answered, "As an individual cable operator I am not satisfied with my own company's progress nor with that of many of the hundreds of individual companies that make up the industry. We have a long way to go."

I made an appointment to see J. Richard Munro, chief operating officer of Time, Inc. Dick's company had just joined the cable industry, and with his clout and commitment I thought he might be helpful as chairman of N.C.T.A.'s committee on equal opportunity. Dick accepted the responsibility and suggested that we cut it down to size by asking every N.C.T.A. department head to hire one minority person during the next twelve months.

Senator Fritz Hollings later attended a board meeting of the N.C.T.A. in Sarasota. He was there, among other reasons, to press for the cable industry's compliance with equal employment opportunity. Through the good offices of Tom Wheeler, the senator invited Gerrie ("the little woman") and me to join him and his wife in playing tennis doubles.

On the way to the court, I whispered into Gerrie's ear, "You've got to play customer tennis. They've got to win." But Gerrie was not about to give the equal-opportunity senator a break. "No way," she said, "that's rank discrimination." To prove her point she slammed the first serve return right at the senator's chest.

Later, with Gerrie at my side, I traveled the country "from

sea to shining sea" for the N.C.T.A. I did not permit a meeting to go by without issuing an appeal to hire more minorities, and I was able to describe to my constituents N.C.T.A.'s commitments: To provide financial support and professional expertise to the American Association of Cable Television Owners, an association created to assist minorities in locating and obtaining CATV franchises and financing; to retain a consulting firm to design a guide to be mailed out to the entire industry, advising members how to comply with the EEO rules and establish their own affirmative-action policies; and to sponsor workshops and panel discussions at state and regional cable association meetings around the country.

Before I became active in N.C.T.A., the words "professional lobbyist" had a negative connotation for me, but because of my experience in Washington, I changed my view of lobbyists and their function. All serious senators and congressmen are overworked and understaffed. They cannot possibly deal with all the demands of their office, so they depend on professional staff to run their offices. Staff members, too, are overworked and spend many a night burning the midnight oil. That is where professional lobbyists enter the scene. They provide congressional staff with information on their clients and, to be effective, they must provide an honest analysis of the issues. The staff recognizes the built-in bias, but a wise staff uses it as just another source of information.

A good lobbyist who develops honest relationships with congressional staff serves an important function in providing one point of view, intelligently and analytically. Most lobbyists are not the flashy influence-peddlers highlighted in the press but are hard-working professionals who play an important function in the interlocking wheels of Washington. When lobbyists overstep that function, it is the result of poor staff work.

During my years as vice-chairman and chairman of N.C.T.A., my mentor at N.C.T.A. was Tom Wheeler. Tom rehearsed every congressional appearance. He prepared me for questions I would be asked by the press or a congressman or the guard at the Senate office building. He made certain I would never be embarrassed by lack of preparation. He reviewed every speech I made and taught me how to stage a public appearance.

Gerrie accompanied me on many of my long-distance travels on behalf of N.C.T.A., but I made so many short trips to Capitol Hill that for a time I felt that I was commuting to Washington. The following conversation took place in our bedroom one night in that twilight zone just before sleep.

"Dan, I hear the squeak of your suitcase; where are you going tomorrow?" Gerrie asked.

"To Washington, dear."

"No, not again. Why this time?"

"To testify before the House communications subcommittee," I explained.

"But you just did that."

"Well, you're right, it is the second time in three months," I admitted.

"They must find you simply fascinating! Don't our congressmen have anything better to do?"

"Oh, you don't understand," I told her. "We testify to Congress, not to congressmen."

"I don't understand. Then who hears the testimony and represents Congress?"

"Karen Possner."

(Karen Possner was a young, ambitious staff member of the House communications subcommittee who had the cable industry at her feet. She directed the hearings and had prepared an "Option Paper" with 565 questions and answers about the cable industry. This gave her tremendous power. Unfortunately, she was basically anti-cable and the wording of many questions she proposed seemed biased).

"Karen Possner," Gerrie remembered—"Isn't she the nice young woman who went antiquing with me at the Florida convention?"

"Yes, dear."

"Oh, is Karen Possner going to ask you questions tomorrow?"

"She has already asked them—565 of them, in something called an Option Paper."

"Then why do you have to go to Washington?"

"Don't ask me so many questions, dear."

In my travels throughout the country I made dozens of speeches rallying the troops. I prepared one generic speech and then tailored it for each region visited. Here are two excerpts from speeches that I gave under the dual title of vice-president, Comcast Corporation, and chairman of the National Cable Television Association. The first is from a speech to the Western Cable Television Show and Convention on November 10, 1977, six months after I became chairman of the N.C.T.A.

A renewed, a regenerated sense of confidence pervades the industry—and for good reason. We are witnesses to the convergence of three significant forces: technology, creativity and deregulation. We follow their respective paths in:

1. The adoption of satellite technology to program distribution for TV cable systems, a development that I believe will, in significance for this industry, outpace any other of this decade.

2. The surge of creativity that has shaped the first new entertainment medium since commercial television: pay cable.

3. A dawning recognition in Washington—some would call it a revelation—that the industry has won its right to parity: by administration stipulation, by congressional legislation, and by F.C.C. regulation.

As a result, this business is becoming fun again!

Look about this country.

You see it in the exuberance of the chief technician, who after a three-day struggle with the Tinker-toy construction of an earth station, turns on first the LNA, then the receiver, fine-tunes the antenna's elevation and azimuth —part of our new vocabulary—and reaches twenty-three thousand miles out into space for a selection, a potpourri, of programming never before at his disposal.

And he knows it is only the beginning.

You see it in the brainstorming sessions that once again play a role in system management. For the first time in years, system operators exercise choice and imagination. Higher earnings are no longer a sole function of rate increases that play hopscotch with inflation, of cost reductions that threaten service, or clawing up that last notch on subscriber saturation.

No! For once we can draw upon an inventory of new services for our subscribers: New products, if you will. Products that can be improved, priced out, packaged, promoted and mechanized to attract subscribers, to generate income.

The products I speak of are of course HBO, Showtime,

Channel 100, Madison Square Garden, Channel 17, Christian Broadcasting network, UPI video New Channel, and the new entry, a video service that will draw upon Time, Inc.'s stable of magazines for its format.

And we know it is only a beginning.

You can see it even in the Washington salons, in the questions asked of industry witnesses by senators, by congressmen, by their staffs. For the first time, you see respect for the industry's accomplishments, an awe for its potential. You see empathy—nay, sometimes disbelief—as they stare into the regulatory abyss into which the F.C.C. has flung the industry.

Even in the F.C.C., there is a turning of the screw, castigated—raked over the judicial coals—by an appeals court that could not perceive "any public benefit to be achieved by hobbling cable television"; urged on by a house communications subcommittee staff report that juxtaposed cable television's promise against the performance of regulators. It is F.C.C. Chairman Wiley who finally admitted that "The F.C.C. has never had an adequate empirical base for projecting potential harm to the broadcast industry from cable competition."

And now after nearly twenty years of the commission's benign neglect of the facts, an economic inquiry has been undertaken. We support this inquiry, but lest it become another strategy for delay, our industry is maintaining the pressure on Washington.

At the F.C.C. it is the filing of a Petition for Rulemaking to eliminate all signal restrictions—distant, syndicated, simultaneous. I consider this by far our industry's single most important deregulatory goal.

In the Congress, it is the submission of a blueprint for rewrite of the communications act, as comprehensive a legislative proposal as has been framed by an industry.

And yet, at best, it is just a beginning!
Yes, our industry is on the move again!

By the following year, the N.C.T.A.—once regarded by broadcasters and Congress alike as a renegade group of outsiders and nobodies—had become influential enough to attract some of Washington's most powerful policy-makers to its annual convention, as I noted in my opening remarks on May 2, 1978:

As we celebrate this industry's thirtieth year and convene our twenty-seventh convention in this charming city of New Orleans, I suggest to you that none of the "crystal-ball gazing" in which we all will participate over the next three days will seem as far-fetched, seem as bereft of reality, seem as readily subject to derision as would the predictions of cable 1978 have been at N.C.T.A.'s first meeting in Pottsville, Pennsylvania, on January 12, 1952.

Imagine Speaker Tip O'Neill, his hair perhaps a few shades darker, his frame a few pounds lighter, but with that same delightful twinkle, predicting in 1952 at the NECHO-Allen Hotel in Pottsville that this industry's thirtieth anniversary would be celebrated with over five thousand convention attendees.

Imagine that the Speaker of the House, the chairman of the Senate and House communications subcommittees, and the chairman of the F.C.C. all would come to New Orleans to address this industry, an industry that:

Has wired one-fifth of the nation;

Provides service to thirteen million homes;

Finally succeeded in that elusive scheme first proposed for radio by Zenith's Commander McDonald, a system that substitutes the viewer's choice for the advertiser's dominance—pay cable, in 1.5 million homes;

Can call upon its own national satellite network;

Is embracing new technologies—fiber optics, lasers, two-way communications, and satellite communications;

An industry that will in its thirtieth year exceed a billion dollars in gross income.

Even that perennial optimist, the chairman of the first N.C.T.A. meeting, Martin Malarkey, would have laughed these predictions right off the podium.

I suggest it is not a fantasy to envision, as this convention examines our industry's next decade:

The deployment of our country's creative resources to conceive new forms of entertainment, new techniques of education, and new channels of community interaction;

The infinite capabilities of fiber optics;

The full exploration of two-way video communications;

The construction of vast urban communication systems.

And yet, at best, it is just a beginning!

Professionals I respected supported my efforts at N.C.T.A. One day, while speaking at the Denver Cable Club, I noticed Bill Daniels in the audience. I asked him to stand, and everyone cheered him.

If Milt Shapp was the intellectual among the industry's pioneers, Bill Daniels was the romantic. He could have stepped right out of an Indiana Jones script. Bill was genuine Americana. In a society where entrepreneurship and salesmanship create icons, he was among the best. A fighter pilot during World War II, he won a bronze star for heroism as a member of the Blue Angels flight team.

In the cable industry Bill Daniels was a trailblazer. He served as one of the early leaders of our national organization, founded the first cable brokerage company, owned hundreds of cable systems and launched the first cable investment banking business. It was at an annual meeting where Bill Daniels made a successful motion to change the cable industry's name from "community antenna system" to "cable television." After all, he said, "You can buy an antenna in any Sears store for less than a hundred dollars, and it certainly didn't belong to the community."

After my presentation in Denver, Bill came up to me to congratulate me. He admitted having had doubts about my ability to fill the post of chairman, but, hearing my presentation, he was convinced I was one of the best chairmen the industry ever had. It would have been a backhanded compliment from anyone else, but from Bill Daniels, it was an honor.

Before my term as chairman expired, a representative of the board sent one of Bill's associates, Marty Rifkin, to urge me to extend my chairmanship for another year. The board was even willing to change the bylaws, which at the time called for a one-year term. Though honored, I declined. Having flown more than fifty thousand miles during the last year on behalf of N.C.T.A., I realized how much time it took away from my business at Comcast. I also knew I would be needed to help in the construction of those "vast urban communication systems" that I had talked about on my trips around the country.

15 *A quantum leap*

When President Jimmy Carter chose a liberal Democrat as F.C.C. chairman in 1977, the cable industry foresaw better times ahead. Charles D. Ferris, a wisecracking, card-playing politician who had served as secretary to the majority leader in the Senate, believed that competition between the cable operators and the broadcasters should replace restrictive legislation. Charles Ferris triggered the end of the era of regulation. By 1984 Congress would pass the Communications Policy Act deregulating the industry.

In a reversal of the trek of American history, the last frontier of the cable-TV industry was America's urban market. After the disappointments of the 1960s and the early 1970s, when a lack of programming and F.C.C. restrictions stunted most urban cable ventures, the acquisition of urban franchises drove the cable industry. In the late 1970s Comcast built its first urban systems: one in Montgomery County, Pennsylvania, serving forty thousand households in four municipalities that adjoined Philadelphia, and another system that reached an equal number of homes in the Meadowlands area of northern New Jersey. The wiring of the urban market was beginning in earnest.

One of Comcast's biggest challenges in the early 1980s was how to introduce pay television to its subscribers. The situation called for new ideas, and it lead to Comcast's biggest marketing program ever. Rather than introduce a single-channel pay service, our strategy was to devise a multi-channel package and to market it as a new tier of service. Included in this new tier were HBO, ESPN Sports, WGN, Nickelodeon, C-Span and several other entertainment and information services. We selected TotalVision as its brand name and marketing umbrella.

For our test audience we picked our largest system, which was located in Flint, Michigan, with more than fifty thousand subscribers spread throughout fifteen communities. By late winter, nearly half of them had selected TotalVision, and we learned two important lessons: Bundling programs worked, and added programming dramatically increased our average income per dwelling. Our viewers enjoyed the bundled programs and were willing to pay extra for them.

By the end of 1980, Comcast's subscribers numbered more than 160,000. For the next two decades our growth would be exponential—half a million subscribers by mid-1985 and double that by the end of the year. In the early 1990s we would be serving more than two and a half million subscribers, and by the millennium that figure would exceed eight million, ranking us as the third-largest cable company in the world, with twenty-five thousand employees.

As our company grew, community involvement remained a top priority at Comcast. Our philosophy was to integrate ourselves into the communities we served. In suburban Phila-delphia, our system broadcast high-school athletics when local TV stations didn't provide coverage. In Trenton, Comcast started a program to hire and train the unemployed in cable construction and installation. In a test program in Clinton, Michigan, and in Paducah, Kentucky, subscribers' water meters were read in a two-way cable hookup. Comcast provided equipment for a community college to produce its own programming. We also encouraged our managers and employees to participate in civic and industrial affairs in the communities they served. Bill Dunlap headed Tupelo's Community Development Foundation and was chairman of the local bank; Howard Barnett volunteered for the board of directors of Meridian's poverty program and joined the board of the Meridian city library. Comcast's responsiveness to the community goes beyond any statutory requirements because community involvement is a corporate responsibility —and good business.

For those who hadn't noticed that the cable-TV industry had grown up and that the launch of communication satellites had revolutionized the way the industry worked, a record-setting auction on November 9, 1981, underscored the point.

In an event respectfully reported by the *New York Times*, representatives of the most powerful members of the communications industry gathered at Sotheby Park Bernet's uptown Manhattan gallery. It could have been a communications summit meeting. In the room were representatives of cable-TV programmers such as HBO, Showtime, and Warner Amex; all three networks, NBC, CBS, and ABC; major broadcasters such as Westinghouse and Viacom; and leading publishers, including Time Inc. and the Times Mirror.

Suspended above them in the gallery auditorium was

an object that could have been a contemporary sculpture. But this object was destined not for a museum, but for the heavens. It was a replica of a satellite, and the fifty bidders who took up Sotheby's black-and-white paddles were competing for leases for seven transponders—transmitters the size of a cigarette carton—that would relay signals from the earth to space and back again from RCA's newest satellite, to be launched the following January.

The opening bid for the first transponder was fifty thousand dollars. The bidding moved quickly and the last paddle was raised at $14.4 million. Bidding for the second transponder opened at one million and rose to $14.1 million. At the end of fifty-six minutes and thirty seconds, seven transponders had brought a total of $90.1 million in winning bids, surpassing the previous record total for a single Sotheby auction by more than fifty-six million dollars. Sotheby president John Marion concluded, in the bland understatement of high society:

"Thank you! At these prices, it would be so nice to have you come back again."[15]

Return we did, because the auction symbolized the revolution in entertainment and communications wrought by cable television.

About that same time, the cable-television industry entered a phase of frenzied franchise application in a race to capture the urban markets that would become the mainstay of the wired nation. Comcast's Philadelphia franchise application, which took twenty years and five applications to shepherd through successive city councils, was not atypical.

On December 22, 1982, each cable franchise was required to submit seventy-five copies of its application. That equaled fifteen hundred binders at a total weight of four and a half tons. The night before, Ralph, Julian and I burned the midnight oil to pack and check the applications, together with our vice-president in charge of franchising, Barbara Lukens, and others.

At eight the next morning, Comcast was the first to deliver its proposals to Philadelphia's Municipal Services Building. As the boxes of proposals were wheeled in and stacked up in the designated tenth-floor room, city officials watched with amazement as one entire wall was filled with Comcast's applications. By mid-morning several other companies arrived, and other walls of the room were obliterated from view. By mid-afternoon, ten tons of paper sat on the floor of that tenth-floor room, and there was concern that the floor might buckle or even collapse. The remaining applicants were quickly instructed to bring only one copy of their application to the tenth floor and leave the rest on the loading dock.

A few weeks later city council held public hearings on cable franchises. Each applicant was invited to describe his proposal and answer questions. I well remember one hearing of the Philadelphia cable committee that was chaired by City Councilman Fran Rafferty. Councilman Rafferty had been a boxer in his youth and was not loath to display his combative nature to his opponents on council. He had reviewed the application of Chuck Dolan, the president of Sterling Information Service, a New York company that was beginning to wire the city of New York, and asked him why he had arranged to include in his group an important Republican politician.

Mr. Dolan replied, "I needed someone to show me my way through Philadelphia." "For that," said Rafferty, "you can hire a Philadelphia cabby who'll do it for twenty dollars."

No decision was made for many months. The approval of franchises for Philadelphia waited until the next mayor, W. Wilson Goode, took office in 1984. Comcast was eventually granted one of the four franchises offered by the city and as part of the agreement, we moved our corporate operations into Center City.

Finally, on July 31, 1986, I sat next to Mayor Goode in the Mayfair section of Philadelphia, at the home of Rick and Terry Lev, when Comcast threw the switch. We made history that day: the Levs, by becoming Comcast's first Philadelphia cable customers, and Comcast, by being the first company to bring modern cable television to Philadelphia. Curiously, we were actually settling cable's last frontier. Comcast later purchased the other Philadelphia franchises and today serves subscribers in a complex that extends from Philadelphia's City Hall toward the northwestern suburbs and into southern New Jersey.

By the middle of the 1980s, cable was entering adulthood. There were already forty million households in America where the words cable and television were interchangeable. Cable had become a major form of entertainment, and, for the first time, an entire generation was growing up on cable. Cable was changing the way we learned about our world. It was educating our children, bringing products to our door and above all, it was helping us to lead better-informed lives without leaving the comfort of our homes and our families.

The days of building one new cable franchise after another was gone forever. The focus shifted from constructing new systems to maximizing the value of systems already built and to acquiring additional properties with significant potential that appeared underdeveloped. A case in point was Comcast's 1985 acquisition of five hundred thousand subscribers from Group W Cable, a subsidiary of Westinghouse Electric Company. Group W Cable fit Comcast's criteria by being a potentially superb, underdeveloped property, offered at a good price. The acquisition enabled Comcast, in a quantum leap, to rise to national prominence by doubling its size and becoming one of the largest cable companies in the country.

Then came new opportunities for expansion in another direction. In the early 1990s, after spending nearly half their business lives trying to squeeze just one more channel out of their analog systems, cable operators had reached a solid wall at fifty-two channels—when suddenly, like a gift from the heavens, along came digital compression. Actually, this transmission technique had been utilized in the cable industry since the mid-1980s, but its impact was not generally recognized until late in the decade.

Digital compression increased channel capacity from fifty-two to five hundred-plus channels and wrought another change in communications: It was equally applicable to satellite transmission, increasing its capacity three-and four-fold. To the cable operator that was a double-edged sword: It increased the capacity of his system beyond his wildest dreams, but the subscriber perceived it as holes to be filled with programming, which at the moment cable did not have.

All the largest operators immediately—if they had not already done so—entered programming production. They bought sports teams, movies, began producing their own shows and became full-fledged broadcasters, not only to satisfy subscriber demands but also to ward off competition from DBS (direct broadband signal), for which direct reception was available at a much lower cost.

The magic number on which the cable future rests is

three: digital compression, satellite distribution and the re-production of product with more and better programming. These three technical revolutions, which three men were among the first to recognize, magically transformed the cable industry from a communications system of scarcity to one of abundance.

The three wise men who were among the first to recognize this technical revolution were Dr. John Malone, Gerald Levin and Ted Turner.

Dr. John Malone is like a giant who strides the earth in seven-league boots, leaving the crowd behind. He immediately saw the opportunity digital compression created for the cable industry and announced that he would order one million digital converters as proof of his confidence. Working with Bob Magness, he built Television Cable Industries (TCI) into the largest cable company in the industry, then sold it to his potential competitor, AT&T. Included in the sale was Liberty Media, a programming and broadband company that was reorganized as a non-affiliated subsidiary of AT&T. After the sale of TCI, Malone reemerged as president and chairman of Liberty Media. He is a brilliant tactician and bright as hell. At the same time he has always been, to me at least, an enigma wrapped in mystery. No one knows where he will appear next. His advice is sought in any major under-taking of the cable industry.

Jerry Levin swam the moat and scaled the walls until he reached the top turret of Henry Luce's empire, Time, Inc. Personally, and with little outside help, he changed the direc-tion of the world's most powerful communications institu-tion. He persuaded one of the country's most prestigious boards of directors to change direction and invest in cable. The day his company sold network stations to buy cable, he got the attention of other media barons as well as Wall Street: They doubted his sanity, but at the same time, they began to learn more about the cable business and started to invest in its future. As an added benefit, Jerry Levin succeeded in winning acceptance for cable TV.

Jerry functions with controlled emotions and his logic is irrefutable. His foresight as it relates to cable has been on the mark. By bringing Time, Inc. into the cable industry, he assured cable's pedigree among his peers. He and Chuck Dolan developed HBO into a major source of added revenue for cable service and brought the silver screen to television.

I first met Jerry Levin when HBO ran out of microwave links and was delayed in reaching its potential audience in western Pennsylvania. Comcast was one of the first systems in western Pennsylvania to add HBO to its program schedule. The other cable operators were hesitant, fearing that HBO would cannibalize their other services. Comcast's order for HBO's services was crucial at the time, for Jerry was under great pressure to speed up the growth of HBO. Later, in traveling around the country during my service as N.C.T.A. chairman, I became convinced that HBO would succeed in becoming an intrinsic part of the subscriber's viewing habits, and I considered it my responsibility to spread the word.

Jerry has been the futurist of the industry. As CEO of AOL Time Warner, which was formed in the largest merger in corporate history, he will be able to fulfill his own predictions.

Ted Turner has the common touch, despite his wealth. He relates well to people of all classes because he knows their tastes and their entertainment preferences. He shares their nostalgia for the silver screen, their identification with professional sports and their obsession with news. That is what has made him one of the most successful programmers in the history of television. He helped fill the empty channels that digital compression created, without which the entire effort would have been in vain. His Atlanta Channel 17 is the most widely carried movie channel on cable. He bought the Atlanta Braves so that he could control his sports-programming source. His all-news network, CNN, has succeeded in being recognized as "the fourth network." The most visible recognition of CNN's standing as the fourth network is the inclusion of its TV anchors in presidential news conferences and all major news events.

Ted Turner is recognized wherever he goes. I saw his popularity first-hand when I hosted a luncheon of the Philadelphia chapter of the Foreign Policy Association at which he spoke. As his host, I met him at the airport, and by the time we approached the Bellevue Stratford Hotel, he wanted to get out at Broad and Locust Streets to walk the last three blocks. What usually is a leisurely five-minute walk took nearly half an hour. Everyone we passed recognized him and stopped to talk, to "press the flesh." Ted reciprocated. It was like accompanying a presidential candidate.

Ted makes his points as emphatically as possible. As chairman of N.C.T.A. I once scheduled a meeting with a senator who favored certain anti-cable legislation. Ted accompanied me, and when he saw that he had not persuaded the senator to accept our recommendation, he said, "Mr. Senator, if that legislation passes, my business will be dead." And to the shock of the senator, he threw himself on the floor, turned on his back and raised one leg in the air. Then with a dramatic gasp, he lowered his leg to the floor.

When the international Olympics committee excluded

the Soviet Union from participation in the 1986 Olympics, Ted Turner, who believed that sports should not be political, decided to sponsor his own international Olympics in Moscow, the Goodwill Games. Gerrie and I attended a luncheon celebrating the event. The speaker's podium was in a tent set up for the occasion. The speakers were President Ronald Reagan, Ted Turner, and Jane Fonda, the politically liberal actress and fitness expert who later became Ted Turner's wife. Probably the only man in the United States who could have bought three people of such wide political diversity under the same tent was Ted Turner. While we were sharing our buffet luncheon, I sneaked a peek at Jane Fonda as she consumed her lunch and saw that it was popcorn that she popped into her mouth, one kernel at a time.

During his extraordinary career Ted Turner has played many roles, and in 2001 he became vice-chairman of AOL Time Warner. Recently asked what role he would like to have played in another era, he replied, "Ride with King Arthur and carry his sword." Ted Turner is a man of many moods, sometimes court jester and at other times the bearer of King Arthur's shining sword.

In his current role, Ted directs his sword at the nuclear threat to civilization. He has formed an advisory board of business leaders who share his convictions that it is possible to bring about worldwide nuclear disarmament. He electrified the world when he donated a billion dollars to the United Nations in 1997. In addition, he supports a foundation that has disbursed more than $250 million to a variety of environmental, population and human-rights projects.

Ted Turner may well be remembered not as the giant of the cable industry he is, but as the man who saved the world. I am proud to have served on the same watch with him.

Comcast's incomparable team: Ralph J. Roberts, chairman, at right, and Brian L. Roberts, president, at the start of the year 2000.

Leading Comcast in new directions for the new millennium: Brian L. Roberts.

Comcast's spectacular growth in the 1980s necessitated changing the company's chain of command from the informal, *gemeutlich* hands-on operation to a more conventional hierarchy. In 1981, in accordance with these changes, my title was upgraded from president of Comcast cable communications to chairman and chief executive officer of the division.

Once there had been a time when I was involved in every major decision involving the operation of each and every one of Comcast's cable systems. Of course, this also had been true for Ralph and Julian, and in fact most people in the company would have been able to say the same for their own areas of responsibility. As that became impossible, some of us heard the voice of a Jewish mother in our heads, expressing two reactions: "No one can do it as well as I," or worse, "If I don't know about it, it obviously isn't being done." Both of these attitudes lead to management atrophy.

It became part of my mission to help manage this new organization by encouraging staff members to accept the responsibilities assigned to them; to assign responsibility, but define those responsibilities lest responsibility merely become a matter of individual perception; and to raise the standards of expectation. Not, "I'll let someone else do it though he will never perform as well as I"; instead, "I expect it to be done as well as I did it, otherwise, I will find people who can."

Time and again, I reminded the Comcast staff, "Don't be shackled by a chain of command. Everyone in this company is at your disposal at any time, from Ralph on down."

As it should be, the younger generation of leaders, who were in their thirties, began to take over the reins. In 1991 I retired from Comcast, and in 1997 I resigned from the board of directors. My longtime Comcast colleague, Abe

Patlove, was right when he said, "Dan, we have become dinosaurs."

The family dynasties in the cable industry disprove the homily that powerful founders choose unworthy successors, although the numbers of dynasties are shrinking, their heirs having been lured by the glitter of gold to sell their companies. The remaining dynasties include Chuck Dolan and his son, James, and Ralph Roberts and his son, Brian. I know Brian Roberts well, having worked side by side with him for nearly ten years when he was a teen-ager. Brian, always ambitious and hard-working, came to the office on Saturdays to perform what he called menial tasks. (In fact, like a son, he borrowed—no, he swiped—the *Playboy* magazines which I had taken away from my three sons, and hidden in my desk.)

Brian became president of Comcast at the age of thirty. He and his father are always mentioned in tandem: Ralph as the font of wisdom, and Brian as the leader of new directions for the company. Brian has become a legend in his own time. With little more than a wink and a smile, he coaxed a billion dollars out of the change purse of the world's richest man, Bill Gates. They both want to encase this globe with a digital, broadband communications network of near-infinite capacity. They are both impatient with the speed at which that network is progressing. That's why they clicked —they double-clicked.

In a recent annual report Brian defined Comcast's position at the start of the new millennium:

Technology, communications and entertainment are all converging, creating unprecedented growth opportunities. Comcast is at the heart of it all. Our powerful cable broadband network is the "fat pipe" that is delivering the digital revolution—and a wealth of new products and services —into millions of homes and businesses. We have built the high-speed, two-way infrastructure that the digital world demands. And we're barely scratching the surface of its capabilities.[16]

16 *The relentless hunter*

Although Comcast's future for the next two decades was one of growth and prosperity, I was to face my greatest challenge when I was diagnosed with Parkinson's disease.

It was in 1980 that I first noticed the change. My body wasn't responding properly. I was sluggish, off balance, and less alert. My doctor said, "You're working too hard. Relax and the symptoms will go away."

But go away they did not. As a matter of fact, they got worse. I began to develop tremors in my left arm and hand which I found difficult to control. At a business meeting in London I finally sat on my hand to control the tremor.

Two more doctors repeated the same mantra, "Don't worry. It is a familial tremor. It will go away."

I then decided that if I am convinced that I have a medical problem and the world assures me that it is not so, I had better see a psychiatrist. The psychiatrist I saw had begun his practice as a neurologist. He asked me to touch my thumb with my index finger in rapid succession. He manipulated my joints. He had me press the palms of my hands against his with full force. Finally, he blindsided me and pushed me off balance.

That done, he turned to me and said, "Dan, you have Parkinson's."

I was shocked, dumbfounded, taken aback. I muttered, "My God, no. Now my life is really out of control."

I was familiar with Parkinson's. I had followed the career of Margaret Bourke-White, the *Life* magazine photographer whose portraits of Gandhi, Stalin, men at war, and the living dead of Buchenwald were some of the great art created during World War II. I was entranced by her photography long before either of us had any notion that both of us had Parkinson's in our future. In an article in *Life,* Bourke-White had announced her resignation from the magazine because she had Parkinson's. In this article she explained the symptoms of "this dreadful disease," and described her bout with Parkinson's in clear, layman's terminology.

James Parkinson, in his *Essay on Shaking Palsy,* first described Parkinson's disease in 1817. The disease strikes two persons in every thousand, usually after the age of fifty. Currently, 1.5 million Americans suffer from this disease. Unfortunately, despite considerable research, the cause of Parkinson's disease still eludes definition.

Researchers do know what happens when Parkinson's strikes. Cells begin dying in a small area of the brain called the substantia nigra. When these cells are healthy, they produce a chemical called dopamine. Dopamine carries messages from cell to cell throughout the brain, the spinal cord and nerves, and out to the muscles. As brain cells die and the supply of dopamine diminishes, a chemical imbalance develops. As a result, parts of the central nervous system do not receive a sufficient supply of dopamine.

Parkinsonism does not affect the thinking part of the brain, but it sabotages the brain's motor centers that coordinate voluntary movements. It is hydra-headed: Push it down in one spot and it rears up in another. It is easy to recognize its two main symptoms, rigidity and tremor.

But to understand what Parkinsonism is, you must know the bewilderment of finding yourself prisoner in your own clothes closet, unable to back out of it.

You must experience the awkwardness of trying to turn around in your own office. It now takes a dozen steps when one swift turnabout used to do the job.

You must live with the near panic you face when you walk into a room full of people, and the uneasiness of the questions you ask yourself:

Do I just imagine that I can't seem to turn over in bed anymore?

How will I get my feet moving when they want to stay glued to the floor?

How will I disengage myself from a group of people and step away if they are all around me? How will I keep from knocking them down?

What can I do with my hands when I am standing still and they shake?

How will I cut my meat? (What a waste of good steak!) You feel so clumsy if you cut it yourself, and so conspicuous if someone does it for you.

How did I look this time? Did I get though it all right, or do people notice that there is anything wrong?"

You must suffer the pangs of finding one day that you can no longer play tennis, your favorite sport, because you're losing your sense of balance, and feel the pain of hanging up your tennis racket as a memorial to the past, while the rest of your family participates in the annual Aaron family tennis tournament.

As soon as I was diagnosed with Parkinson's, Gerrie and I went public. It was such a relief for both of us. My worst fears never materialized; my friends, rather than avoiding us, paid more attention to us and became very supportive. Once we had gone public we were amazed at how many people suffer from Parkinson's. I began to feel comfortable discussing my illness, particularly in a support group that we joined at the Movement Disorders Center at the Graduate Hospital in Philadelphia.

At one session, my support group wrestled with what the writer Susan Sontag calls the *Illness as Metaphor* — the social perceptions, the prejudices and the taboos surrounding illness. The metaphor for Parkinson's is aging. Not only does Parkinson's most commonly affect men and women over fifty, but its symptoms mimic the aging process: stooped posture, halting movement, loss of agility and slurred speech. That poses both social and economic barriers in a youth-oriented society. The Movement Disorders Center is devoted to liberating the illness from its metaphor. The center helps patients to structure and deploy a support system that at its most effective includes the physician, the family, friends, business associates and the employer. That's the task to which the MDC is committed. Its slogan: "Accommodation, not surrender."

It didn't take me long to realize that Parkinson's disease is like a hunter: It stalks its prey. Relentlessly! Once in its sight, there is no escape. It captures its victim's every function —without warning, without pity. As the disease progresses, simple tasks become challenges; handwriting becomes small and cramped; arms don't swing freely when walking. Walking becomes difficult, and in initiating that first step, one becomes frozen in place. My invention of a specialized cane that has a bar at the bottom, attached at a right angle, is a help. It tricks my mind into thinking something is in the way of my foot, an object I have to step over. It helps to get me "unfrozen" and moving.

In a sense, the patient can more easily control the physical manifestations of the disease, particularly in its early stages, than the psychological, social and economic consequences.

Fortunately, my disease progressed slowly, and I was able to work productively for more than ten years after my diagnosis, until my retirement in 1991. My secretary, Marie Molchen, who joined my office in 1985, was not aware that I had Parkinson's when she first started to work with me. But she soon suspected that something was amiss. As she took dictation from me across from desk, she would hear my foot involuntarily start thumping with a tap, tap, tap. One day, I dictated a letter on the subject of Parkinson's and she realized I was a Parkinson's patient. I was then in the early stages of the disease, and it was a point of pride for me that I never missed a meeting, an appointment, a speech or any other business because of my disability.

Most of the projects in which I was active at that time involved Abe Patlove. Abe was my director of development and later vice-president of the cable division. He was the most loyal of business associates, and had worked with me longer than anyone else, following me from Jerrold Electronics. His attributes included great organizational skills and the ability to take a complicated assignment, break it down into its parts and then assume operating responsibility to get the job done. And Abe had a gift that I lacked: He could remember names. Before a meeting, Abe would quiz me on the attendees, and, once there, a diagram of where people were sitting appeared at my place.

Abe also was mercilessly honest with me; he told me I was the cheapest person he ever knew. That well might be true, but whenever tough negotiations were needed, I would be called on to squeeze the last one percent. We used to say, "Squeeze the eagle until he screams."

After my retirement, Abe was very sensitive to the limitations Parkinson's imposed during the later stage of my illness. He was always the first to offer to drive me to a meeting, help me gather the information I needed, and was always looking over my shoulder to make certain the outline for the meeting I chaired was in order. He made certain I got to the meetings on time. He helped me organize the Dan Aaron Parkinson's Disease Foundation, and volunteered to be an officer and a member of its board. Abe has been at my side whenever I needed him.

In 1982, under the auspices of the American Parkinson's Disease Association, two young neurologists, Dr. Howard Hurtig and Dr. Matthew Stern, joined by Gwyn Vernon, a trained community-health nurse, set up the Parkinson's Movement Disorders Center at Graduate Hospital at Ninth and Pine Streets in Philadelphia. It would become a model that others would emulate.

My close relationship with Dr. Hurtig through the years has been one of mutual admiration. His untiring devotion and dedication to the welfare of his patients is legendary. Balancing medication so that I am able to function is not an easy task, for the disease's progress differs with each patient. Using medication is a process of trial and error; an imbalance can cause hallucinations or equally frightening consequences. Fortunately, Howard Hurtig has been able to find the right combination. He has become not only my physician, but also a good friend.

Early in my treatment it became apparent that the Movement Disorders Center needed a controlling body of lay leaders, a board of directors who could raise funds for the center's programs and at the same time promote public awareness of Parkinson's. So Gerrie and I created the Greater Philadelphia Parkinson's Council. In 1989, after a series of bike-a-thons and walk-a-thons, we held our first gala, honoring the three founders of the center. We were pleased to realize over fifty thousand dollars from our efforts.

In 1991, the year I retired as vice chairman of Comcast, the Parkinson's Disease and Movement Disorders Center of the Graduate Hospital named me Man of the Year. This meant a fund-raiser in my honor and the establishment of the Dan Aaron Parkinson's Disease Foundation.

In a letter sent over my signature to the giants of the cable industry, to my friends at Comcast, and to the public, I asked for support for this new foundation. I was amazed when my longtime secretary, Marie Molchen, told me that the dinner to be held at the Ritz Carlton Hotel in Philadelphia was oversubscribed and that more than five hundred people wanted to attend.

The gala evening opened with comments from Ralph Roberts, who cited the Movement Disorders Center as an outstanding example of how private citizens can join together with a major institution to provide new health programs for those afflicted with debilitating disease.

Expressions of support arrived from all over the country, including a letter from President George Bush.

THE WHITE HOUSE

WASHINGTON

September 25, 1991

Dear Mr. Aaron:

Because our nation's greatness will be measured
less by our wealth than by our willingness to
help others, I am delighted to have learned of
your generosity and hard work on behalf of your
fellowman.

You have earned the admiration of your friends
and neighbors through your commitment to the
values that have made our nation great -- duty,
sacrifice, and a patriotism that finds its
expression in voluntary community service. Your
efforts to help people who suffer from Parkinson's
disease illustrate how each of us can make a
difference in the lives of others, how each of us
can be a shining "Point of Light" in our community.
I commend you for your achievements.

Barbara joins me in wishing you continued success
and every happiness in the future. God bless you.

Sincerely,

George Bush

The evening was a success: We raised more than four hundred thousand dollars for the Dan Aaron Parkinson's Disease Foundation. Before the turn of the century, two more galas were held with equal success.

In the year 2000, at the beginning of the millennium, our fund-raising efforts focused on building a new rehabilitation center, an extension of the Movement Disorders center. On November 16, 2000, the Dan Aaron Parkinson's Rehabilitation Center was dedicated. The mission of the center is to provide to Parkinson's patients, their families, and caregivers the education, the rehabilitation, the counseling, and the socialization skills that will allow them to achieve higher levels of functioning and an improved quality of life. The center provides space for a large gymnasium, equipment to allow patients to practice their skills in activities of daily living, and meeting rooms for Parkinson's support groups.

Jane Wright, program coordinator at the center, reports that "The money that has been raised for the center by Dan over the years has been put to good use. The center currently supplies professional help to forty support groups throughout the tri-state area, going as far north as Scranton, south into Delaware, east into New Jersey and as far west as Penn State. The center regularly publishes the *Transmitter,* a multi-page bulletin that brings patients up-to-date information on Parkinson's, and funding also is used for new programs to make minority groups aware of services available for Parkinson's patients."

In the last two decades I have developed these Ten Commandments for dealing with Parkinson's:

1. *Remember that the patient gets the attention; the caregiver bears much of the burden.*

The caregiver can easily become the substitute target of all the resentment, hostility and anger borne by the patient against the disease. This can threaten the relationship between mates. It can undermine the support ordinarily supplied by the patient's children, and it can only increase the feeling of guilt the patient carries for his responsibility in this emotional turmoil.

Make certain that the same tolerance shown to the patient is extended to the caregiver. Give the caregiver the proper credit for his or her sacrifices.

2. Don't feel sorry for yourself. Forget it!

Is Parkinson's the worst thing that could happen to you? Probably not! Try to be tough.

3. Maintain a sense of humor.

The discomforts caused to others by the disease can often be eased by humor. Have some humorous remarks ready which you can inject as tense situations arise.

Entrance into a restaurant that lacks a ramp for wheelchairs and therefore requires you to maneuver or be carried up steps will turn every head in your direction. That is a good time to think of something funny.

For example, I like to tell other Parkinson's patients about a story that appeared in the *New York Times* reporting that researchers are using fruit flies to study Parkinson's disease. Because fruit flies multiply so rapidly, they provide much faster research results than other lab animals. I warned everyone who has Parkinson's to think twice before they swat a fly, because "The life you save might be your own."

Remember, laughter dissipates embarrassment, reduces strain, and calms your stomach.

4. Involve your entire family.

Whenever we invite children of patients to join sessions of our support group, the most often-repeated complaint is, "My parents won't discuss it. They pretend everything is OK when we know it just ain't so. By not sharing their hardships with us, they build a wall between us."

5. Exercise, exercise, and exercise.

No matter what your limitations, the most important single activity, second to none, is exercise.

A sweaty brow covers many ills.

6. Don't let your daydreams turn into nightmares.

Force yourself to turn your daydreams into positive thoughts. Don't dwell on the miseries of Parkinson's. This has to be a consciously controlled effort; otherwise you may lapse into feeling sorry for yourself.

Many experts argue that depression is a symptom of Parkinson's, and this is an ongoing debate. It seems to me that having Parkinson's is enough reason to be depressed. No matter! Depression should be treated with the help of professionals.

A new project of the Dan Aaron Parkinson's Disease Foundation is to explore depression as related to Parkinson's disease. The Beck Institute at the University of Pennsylvania, using cognitive therapy, will monitor this research.

7. Get involved.

Don't bury your head in the sand. Join as many activities with others as you can.

8. Don't hide in the closet.

Go public.

The symptoms of Parkinson's, particularly dyskinesia, which is a lack of muscle control, are unsightly and ungainly. They freeze facial expressions and distort movements. They are ugly! By hiding and not revealing to anyone who expresses an interest that you have Parkinson's, you only force others to speculate and misinterpret the truth.

9. Join a support group.

You're not alone, and what you can learn from a support group will surprise you.

10. Keep on fighting!

And remember—there is hope!

It is estimated that Parkinson's disease costs the United States twenty-five billion dollars or more annually. Although the Morris K. Udall Parkinson's Disease Research Act of 1997 called for government spending of a hundred million dollars a year for research, the disease receives far less support per individual patient than most other major disorders.

Parkinson's is progressive and cannot be cured; however, its symptoms can be effectively treated. Because Parkinson's progresses slowly, successful treatment by medication such as Sinemet can control the symptoms for many years and allow patients to lead active and independent lives. Hopefully, research such as that carried on at the Movement Disorders Center, now a part of Pennsylvania Hospital, may find improved means of treatment during the years ahead and make it possible to keep the symptoms reasonably in abeyance for the remainder of a patient's life.

In recent years Michael J. Fox, the remarkable actor who retired from *Spin City* because of his Parkinson's, boxer Muhammad Ali, and Janet Reno, the former U.S. Attorney General, have publicized the need to allocate substantial money for research, and others need to encourage Congress to act. I would be delighted to return to Washington once again to testify before Congress—this time, to appeal for more resources to fight this predatory disease.

17 *Closing the circle*

One day in 1978 I received an astonishing letter from Germany. It announced the publication of a "History of the Jewish People of Giessen," subsidized by the state and authored by a Professor K. As I had had no contact with Germany in more than forty years I was astounded by this example of German efficiency and puzzled over how anyone could have discovered my connection with Giessen. I sent for the report.

The study traced the Jewish residents of Giessen back to the Middle Ages. According to the report, they had worked as moneylenders and as cattle and grain traders. At regular intervals during the intervening years, the Jews of Giessen had been ordered to leave the walled city. After a short stay on the outside, they would be allowed to return to their homes once they paid a special "protective tax."

By 1933, the Giessen Jewish community had grown to thirteen hundred members whose religious affiliation was divided between the Reform and Orthodox synagogues. At this time, they were active in the business, medical, legal, banking and teaching professions. Teachers taught at both the undergraduate and graduate level, with many of them occupying professorships at the University of Giessen.

The study traced the place of birth, occupation and destination of each of the thirteen hundred members of the Giessen Jewish community from 1933 until 1942. In 1942 Giessen's remaining two hundred Jews were marched to the town square on the way to the concentration camps from which none returned.

It was in this compilation that I first learned the fate of two of my first cousins, Clara and Menn. The day before they were ordered to gather in the town square for a final trip to the concentration camp, Theresienstadt, they had drowned themselves in the local river, Lahn.

In 1933, 650,000 members of the Jewish faith lived in Germany. Statistically, 60 percent of these escaped the horrors that were to follow, while 40 percent did not. Giessen's Jews, in terms of percentage, met the same fate.

Professor K.'s report stirred feelings within me that I could not ignore. I wanted to know what had happened to my family and to the friends who had been part of my childhood in Giessen.

Among the relatives about whom I did have information was my mother's family, the Bergmanns. They lived in Fuerth, a suburb of Nuremberg, a large industrial city in the southern part of Germany. The Bergmanns had been successful traders in hops, a vital ingredient in the production of beer. They would buy the hops crop as it ripened in the fall, dry it through the winter and sell it in the spring to small breweries throughout Germany and the world.

According to family legend, my great-uncle Bergmann immigrated to the United States in 1850. Instead of getting off the transatlantic steamer in New York, he continued the voyage to Portland, Oregon, established a successful business and eventually was elected mayor of Portland.

Among our Fuerth relatives were the Speers, who conceived, manufactured and sold table games. During the industrial revolution of 1850, they built one of the first German toy factories, and during the intervening years became one of Germany's largest toy manufacturers. Their most famous product was Scrabble, and to this day they retain the rights to the game. By the time Hitler confiscated their facilities they had moved their operations to England, where they are currently living.

Of the rest of our family or friends I knew nothing. I felt I had to return to Giessen to close the circle. It would be thirteen years before I would fulfill my wish, but after my retirement in 1991, I was determined to return to my place of birth.

Memory works like binoculars. To focus an image through binoculars, one slowly adjusts the lens until all is clear. To remember, one searches one's mind for memories of the past and slowly defines and redefines that memory. But unlike an event seen through binoculars, once a memory comes into focus, it is often hard to distinguish fact from fiction. Added to all of this was the fact that more than fifty years had passed, blurring my image of Giessen.

As I thought about my return to the place of my birth, one of my more vivid memories of Giessen was the Sunday walks that Frank and I took with our parents through the pine woods that surrounded our town. All the paths had markings that we could follow to a destination of our choice; a red arrow led to a beer *stube* (a beer hall), a yellow circle to a local castle built during the Middle Ages, and a green marking led to the lake. As we started our sojourn through

*For boys like Frank and me, the
woods near Geissen were filled
with adventure.*

the woods Frank and I would choose our destination and
challenge our parents to a race to see who would get there
first. It was an exciting game that could take all day, and
many times we were out well after dark.

As memories came flooding back, a childhood friend,
Jost Fuhr, came to mind. His family had owned a toy store
in town, a business that had been in the family for a hundred
years. I decided to call him. Modern technology being what
it was by the early 1990s, finding his telephone number was
no problem for the overseas operator. Remarkably, within
minutes I was connected to his home and we were conversing. My opening statement was to introduce myself:

"Hello, I am Dan Aaron. I am sure you don't remember who I am?"

"I certainly do," was Jost's answer, "we were classmates and very good friends in school."

As I told him of my intent to return to Giessen, he said he would be happy to make arrangements for my visit. He said he would include another one of our classmates, Fritz Carl, in the planning. Once again jogging my memory, I could honestly say, "Oh yes, I remember Fritz Carl."

In September 1991, Gerrie and I began our trip to Germany, along with Marcia Baum, the wife of Aunt Bertha Katz's grandson. Marcia is the genealogist of our family and brought with her a collection of letters, photographs and memorabilia which she thought might be helpful during our visit to Giessen.

When Fritz Carl met us in Giessen, we were greeted by a jovial, *gemuetlicher* German. He stepped forward and greeted me with a friendly smile and expressed his delight in seeing me once again. He exceeded me both in height and girth, and he could not have been a more pleasant tour guide. His English was excellent; he had taught English in one of the local schools prior to becoming its principal.

Fritz Carl was kind enough to be our guide and chauffeur for the two days we spent in my native city. We met his wife, visited his home, and met his son, who was practicing law. Interestingly, when his son had begun his legal career in Berlin, he was asked to defend clients who had been accused of being Nazis. This created a personal conflict which he resolved by terminating his German law practice and spending several years in a kibbutz in Israel. We talked at length about our respective families, but never came to grips with the Holocaust.

I remember Fritz Carl as a fellow student whose mother was a widow and who tailored men's clothing for a living. Our friendship had been forged because both of us had been ostracized by our classmates, Fritz because of his mother's employment and I because I was "the Jew."

Fritz and I spent two and a half years in school together until, as he put it, one day I just wasn't in school and never reappeared. Fritz went on to graduate with our class, was drafted into the navy, and became an officer. At the end of the war he and two of his fellow officers decided they would become teachers, hoping to instill in future students an understanding of the futility of war.

The gymnasium we had both attended had been bombed during the war and was now reconstructed. We visited the Goethe Elementary School, where we had started our schooling. We walked along the river Lahn where we had ice-skated in the winter and had swum in the summer, and where my two cousins had later committed suicide. When I mentioned to Fritz Carl that I had discontinued both ice-skating and swimming when signs were posted "Jews Not Welcome Here," he expressed surprise; he said he had not seen the signs. For the first time I noticed his discomfort, which appeared every time I mentioned my persecution in Germany. I kept the following memory to myself:

On my first day in elementary school we underwent a physical exam, and the nurse, comparing my height to a chart, shouted so that every student could hear, "The Jew is one centimeter too short." That description taunted me throughout my school career. I was more upset at my physical deficiency than the religious defamation. Perhaps that's how children adjust?

While driving around town, Fritz Carl and I looked for

homes of old school chums and were able to identify a number of them. One of them was that of a Jewish classmate who perished with his family in one of the concentration camps. His father had been a wealthy banker whose bank was attached to his home, and their house had been the envy of the neighborhood. During the war the Gestapo claimed the property for its headquarters. Other homes were no longer standing; the Allied forces had destroyed them in 1942. Unable to hit their prime target of Frankfurt, they had dropped their bombs on their secondary target, Giessen.

The site of the destroyed Reform synagogue was across the street from the stately city theater. The synagogue had been burned on *Kristallnacht* in the fall of 1938. When the remaining Jews tried to collect fire insurance coverage for the building, they received a letter, of which I saw a copy, that said, "It is not possible that the Third Reich would permit the incineration of a synagogue. Since it could not have happened, we are not responsible for this insurance claim."

In 1942, Giessen's two hundred remaining Jewish residents received the order to gather in the town square; they were taken to the gymnasium of the local high school to spend the night there before their trip to Theresienstadt. Later, the principal billed the SS for housing two hundred Jews overnight, but the bill was never paid; according to the SS, it was the school's duty to absorb the cost since it helped "cleanse" Giessen of its Jews.

With Fritz Carl's help, I also found the apartment house where my Uncle Elias and his wife and two maiden daughters had lived. Uncle Elias had lived in America in the twenties and there established a wholesale potato business; at the insistence of his wife, he had returned to Giessen to become a "lap dog" for his wife and two daughters. Both he and his wife died of natural causes; his daughters, unfortunately, did not.

Before leaving Philadelphia, I had arranged to meet with Professor K., the author of the study that had inspired my return to Giessen. While touring Giessen I mentioned my upcoming appointment only to be warned by my friends that the professor's father had been a well-known Nazi lawyer and that his son, the professor, was not to be trusted. So when I met the professor, I was suspicious; he was an energetic, overly friendly man who smiled too much. He reminded me of the line from *Hamlet:* "That one may smile, and smile, and be a villain."

Though he had not recognized my name when I spoke to him by phone, he greeted me by telling me that his father, the attorney, had known my father and had often spoken of him.

During our conversation I discovered that in collecting his information, he had first drawn upon a list that had been compiled by the city government and which he had, by pure chance, found in a cupboard. To bring that list up to date, the professor had advertised in an Israeli publication that was read by German refugees and in a similar publication, the *Aufbau,* published in New York. He told me that he had made a trip to Israel and that he had become an expert on the Holocaust. However, he had never heard of Elie Wiesel. Even more disturbing was his identification of any Jewish name by a number alone. Thus, when I inquired about an old friend, Bruno Oppenheimer, he responded, "Oh yes, that is number 122; he lives in Israel and is a good friend of mine." I began to feel like a character in a Franz Kafka novel.

Before I left the meeting, Professor K. invited me to return to Giessen as a guest of the community. This is a common practice among German cities as a public-relations gesture. I turned down the invitation; I did not want to be a "court Jew," the name given to the few Jews who had held selective posts in the royal court. However, I said I would return at my own expense if granted permission to address the local student body on the subject of the Holocaust. Then he asked that I write to the *Ober Buergermeister* to praise his report and to mention that the report had inspired me to return to Giessen; he explained that this would help his career. As we said our goodbyes, I almost clicked my heels. I never heard from him again.

Our mutual friend, Jost, invited us to his house for a *gemuetlich* dinner where we reminisced about bygone days and caught up with the happenings of the intervening fifty-five years. Jost and his family ran a successful toy store in town and had traveled extensively. His well-appointed apartment over the store displayed many artifacts from his travels. After a delicious meal prepared by his wife, Jost rose for a toast as the dessert plates were being cleared. He was moved to tears as he toasted the bonds of our friendship that sprang from our shared roots in Giessen.

After two days, the thrill of reenacting my youth gave way to the sober realization that the Giessen I now saw was an empty hull, a city without a soul, void of the vibrant Jewish community of which I had been a part. I left with a heavy heart.

Gerrie and I then joined a group of Americans for a guided motor-coach tour of the country. Our tour extended from the Swiss border on Germany's southern fringe to Hamburg and the Baltic Sea on its northern border. Most of the forty-seven tourists in our group were Christians who lived in America's Midwest, and most of them were members of professions: retired teachers, businessmen, a lawyer, and an airline flight attendant. Our means of transportation was a late-model, German luxury bus. A schedule that started at six in the morning and lasted until after dark took us to more than a dozen cities.

Our tour leader, Wilfred, was a long-haired, stylish man of thirty-two who was steeped in German history and who had perfected his fluent English by attending an American private school. Throughout the trip, Wilfred gave us a running commentary on what we were seeing. He hardly mentioned the Holocaust in his historical, sociological and political analysis of Germany. He did not consider it a historic event worthy of much mention. It wasn't a matter of not knowing; it became obvious to me that he didn't want to discuss it. He was much more comfortable telling us about the width, depth and length of a lake, or the size and materials used in a particular statue, or the damage done by Allied bombing to the cities we visited. My fellow travelers, who asked a variety of questions about German history and culture, did not once mention the Holocaust.

During our two days in Munich, our schedule called for a one-day excursion to Oberammergau, the site of the famous Passion Play. Performed every ten years, the Passion Play depicts the life of Christ, from birth to resurrection. (The play, which was virulently anti-Semitic for centuries before Hitler, has been drastically rewritten since the war.) Instead Gerrie and I opted to go to Dachau, one of Germany's largest concentration camps, and invited anyone else who was interested to come with us. A young lawyer from Indianapolis and an African-American flight attendant joined us.

Seeing Dachau was shattering and infuriating. From the

outside the complex looked like a summer camp in the Pocono Mountains of Pennsylvania, except that the administration building, imitating the grand style of a royal palace, was made of sturdy cement block and beautifully whitewashed.

Inside the electric wire fencing, the horrors were all there: the crematorium, the hanging room, and the showers where millions lost their lives.

The state government of Bavaria had built a museum there. I was appalled to find that instead of an accurate portrayal of what had happened in this hellish death camp, the museum was devoted to Hitler's rise to power. There were newspaper articles and publications, cartoons of the period, even photographs of Dachau and its inmates, all focused on a history of Germany. The main victims of the Holocaust, the Jews of Europe, were hardly mentioned. It was obviously a history of Germany, not, as it should have been, a history depicting the tragedy of the Jews. The Order of Carmelites built the only memorial erected in Dachau and dedicated it to reconciliation. It appears to me that reconciliation is an option available only to the victim, not to the criminal perpetrator.

It could not have been an oversight that, in a country where history is an unending calculation of statistics, I could not find a count of the number of Jews who perished at Dachau. I wanted especially to find that number because I wished to discuss my visit to Dachau with the other members of the tour.

When our group returned to Munich, I asked Wilfred if I could share my experience at Dachau with the rest of the group. He agreed reluctantly and added that their reaction would be my responsibility, not his.

I started my tale by briefly describing Dachau. Then I

told them of the following dream I had had the previous night in that twilight zone between wakefulness and sleep. Or was it a dream? I began by telling them:

"Imagine that our group of fifty middle-class husbands, wives and children traveling across Germany in a modern, comfortable, air-conditioned bus were instead jammed into a cattle car with just enough room to sleep standing up. Nazis had rounded us up the night before, banging on the doors of our houses as we slept and demanding that we dress and prepare ourselves for 'resettlement.' We were told to take just the essentials and a few precious heirlooms with us to the local train station for departure.

"The scene quickly changed. This was no excursion or holiday departure. To our dismay, the train station was filled with cattle cars, not passenger cars. As we proceeded to the platform, we noticed that those ahead of us were being relieved of their baggage and forced into cattle cars, prodded by Nazi storm troopers with rifles at the ready and fierce-looking, barking dogs on their leads. One false step of resistance and a bullet would find its mark.

"After leaving the station we endured a train ride for days, sometimes weeks, destination unknown. Once at Dachau we were told to quickly disembark.

"Sick, starving and smudged with urine and feces, we arrived at night to be greeted by more howling, barking dogs and screaming storm troopers. The floodlights of the camp blinded us as the commandant, using his cane, separated us into two lines, one for the elderly, the sick, and the women and children, the other for the men, the young and fit. As I was frantically looking for my wife, I was thrown back into line and told to undress for a shower. I found my wife and the other members of our tour and, together, all of us went into the 'showers.' We waited for the luxury of a hot shower only to hear the hissing of gas effusing from the showerheads. As the poison permeated the entire room, some of us, in a desperate lunge for life, clawed our way up the cement walls. Our prints can still be seen."

The effect of my report on Dachau was beyond what I had hoped. It is hard to believe that most of my fellow tourists knew little of the Holocaust; one of them, the day before, had stated that most concentration camp victims had died of disease and illness. With choked voices, many with tears in their eyes, they thanked me for my talk; some offered sympathy in some form, usually accompanied by a touch.

Before our tour ended and we were about to go our separate ways, a retired Californian came up to me, and, as he took my hand in his, he said, "You finally put the Holocaust into perspective. And you did so in so few words. I'll always remember your face."

I recall this not as a tribute to my eloquence, but to share my astonishment at how little this group of American Christians from all over the United States knew or understood about the Holocaust.

One might ask, How did I survive? My answer:

I was driven to succeed. I always forged ahead, and each tribulation posed a new challenge.

I never became embittered, but I always gained wisdom; yet I always walked in the shadow of the Holocaust.

Had I acted on my foreboding of my parents' imminent death, I might have saved their lives.

Irrational? Yes!

But so was the Holocaust.

After World War II ended, Rabbi Charles Mantinband left

Aberdeen, Maryland, where he had been the U.S.O. administrator, and accepted the pulpit of the Reform congregation in Hattiesburg, Mississippi, from 1952 to 1963. He became a leader in the civil rights movement in the deep South, where he earned a burning cross on his front lawn, constant surveillance by the White Citizens Council, and a barrage of threatening telephone calls warning him, "We know where you are. Get out of town." After enduring eleven years of this harassment, he left Hattiesburg. Successive pulpits in the South followed until his death in 1974.

At his funeral, his widow, my Aunt Anna, said of him, "The record must stand of a man of great spiritual stature who, like the literary figure Abou Ben Adhem, loved his fellow man with grace, with humor and compassion, and, when times demanded it, with unswerving courage."

I said, silently, "Amen."

My brother Frank volunteered for the Korean War during his third year at the University of Alabama. He had received all his shots for overseas duty and was about to be shipped out when the army noticed he had majored in psychology and sociology. Needing soldiers to work in their newly established mental-hygiene clinics, the army had held Frank stateside to fill its need. He became part social worker, part male nurse.

After his stint in the army, Frank returned to school and earned his degree at the University of Texas in Dallas. Several years later, he joined his University of Alabama classmate, Marvin Shwiff, in establishing a home building and development business in Dallas. He married an attractive Englishwoman, Tony Singer, and they have two grown children, Barry and Sharon.

When my eldest son, Jimmy, wanted to go into the building business, it was Frank who took him under his wing and trained him. Thanks to his Uncle Frank, Jimmy now runs his own successful construction business.

Frank and I are very close, but our relationship is a difficult one. We are in constant contact, but we have always felt uncomfortable talking about the deaths of our parents. We never felt emotionally free to question it. As a result, we have never discussed the single most important event in our lives.

For over sixty years, that single most important event in my life has been a subject I kept buried. It wasn't until I began writing these memoirs that I knew I had to seek some answers.

Dr. Aaron T. Beck of the University of Pennsylvania, a world-renowned psychiatrist, the father of cognitive therapy and a friend, helped me explain to myself my delayed bereavement reaction:

Friends have asked me from time to time about my behavioral reactions to my parents' suicides. Some expect that I should recall deep feelings of pain that have persisted over the years.

Actually, my main feeling was numbness—perhaps similar to the kind of shell shock that a soldier experiences.

Why don't I recall having horrible pangs of loss or anger over being abandoned?

Picture a thirteen-year-old boy having lost both his parents and having no one to turn to for consolation and support. Nowadays there are bereavement counselors who specialize in helping survivors of suicides.

I was faced with two choices: Cave in, or pull together the broken pieces. By detaching myself emotionally from the disaster, I was able to take charge of my life and move on.

I suppose I paid a price by shutting off my emotions, but in this way I could reconstitute myself and survive.

I also suppose this experience made me more resilient

when later I encountered other adversities. Possibly, knowing that I could draw on my resources helped me to cope with the worst experience of my adult life—the development of Parkinson's disease.

Slowly my world is closing in on me. I'm reminded of Edgar Allan Poe's short story, *The Pit and the Pendulum,* in which the narrator is imprisoned in a pit beneath a huge pendulum with razor-sharp edges that is swinging back and forth, moving closer with each motion.

My illness is changing my habits. When looking for a restaurant, the quality of the meal is less important than the availability of a handicap ramp. For forty-five years, Gerrie and I have enjoyed going to the Friday afternoon concerts at the Academy of Music in Philadelphia. It was here that we first held hands. We recently turned in our subscription because the entranceway for the disabled leads to underground corridors too difficult to traverse with a wheelchair.

It wasn't until I finished this manuscript that I noticed that not once had I used the word "cripple," which really describes my present condition. Yet in my mind's eye, I see myself as I was twenty years ago, in good health and in good spirits. How I feel is more important than how I look.

As I look back on the last seven decades, to take the measure of my life and my career, the honor of which I am most proud, of all the honors I have received, is the Vanguard Award, which was presented to me in 1987 by the National Cable Television Association. The men and women who are selected for this national award are "people who excel in both business and personal commitment to their colleagues" and to human rights, employee development and encouragement of minority involvement in the industry.

When I joined the cable-television industry, it was the right time; it was the right place. I was there at the beginning —the beginning of an industry, the beginning of a great company. What a rare privilege!

I was carried aloft by the forces of a new industry, and I shared this great adventure with peers, acquaintances and friends of a lifetime: with Gerrie, who raised a family as I lived out of a suitcase and who joined me on my year's road trip as N.C.T.A chairman; with our five children; with my associates at Comcast, particularly Ralph Roberts and Julian Brodsky; and with Milton J. Shapp, who took me into this industry.

Ralph, Julian and Milt, together with so many others of my colleagues, have taught this sometimes-recalcitrant pupil that all is possible.

Given refuge from the Holocaust some sixty years ago, I will always remember that this could only have happened in the land of the free.

Having been a victim of anti-Semitism in Germany, where anti-Semitism was traditionally public policy long before Hitler laid the groundwork for the Holocaust, I am particularly sensitive to any trace of anti-Semitism. During my career I spent time in every part of the United States and competed in many communities against local residents for cable-TV franchises, and I never was conscious of anti-Semitism. Nevertheless, as long as the Jewish community is living in the Diaspora (spread throughout the world), we will continue to be threatened in the future as we have been in the past. That's the lesson we must learn from history. That's why Elie Wiesel shouts from the rooftops for all to hear, "Never Again."

Afterword

As I completed this memoir, I asked my grown children to add some of their own thoughts. What was it like growing up on Marion Road with Dad at the helm? These reminiscences by Erika, Jimmy, Kenny, Jud and Alison are arranged in the birth order of the contributors. Although I was sorely tempted, I did nothing to edit or temper these recollections.

Erika, a nurse practitioner who works with HIV patients at a large hospital in Philadelphia:

The Pine Beach Yacht Club in Toms River, New Jersey, was a day's trip from Marion Road. Members called it a yacht club but it really was just a place where those who loved to sail could put their boats in the water. Dad's first sailboat was a day-sailer that we trailered back and forth from Philadelphia. It was big enough for the entire family, including my baby sister, Alison.

Dad thought sailing would be a fun activity for the whole family, but he didn't have a clue as to how to sail. Fortunately, Dad had a very good friend who was an excellent sailor and who gave him a primer on the art of sailing. I learned how to sail by default.

Dad would take all five kids and put them in the boat, stuffing the younger ones under the deck. Three of us were still in diapers. Before casting off from the safe portals of our yacht club into the cool waters of Toms River, our captain would hand the instruction manual, *The Small-Boat Sailor's Bible,* to me. As the eldest and the only one who could read, it was my duty to answer the questions demanded by the captain:

"How do we come about?"

I would flip to the proper page and read. Once the question was answered, Dad would say, "All right, we are going to do it now. Ready about? Hard to lee." He would then throw the tiller over hard, bringing the boat into the wind and proceed on another tack.

Learning how to jibe was more difficult, for if it was not controlled, the skipper could easily capsize the boat. I would work the jib and Dad would work the mainsail, and fortunately we had no disasters.

And so it went until the captain became a proficient sailor. We soon graduated from our original day-sailer into something larger, finally ending up with a Mariner, a twenty-one-foot vessel that had a cockpit and deck.

I also played a lot of tennis with Dad, who really taught me how to play the game. He had a wicked forehand. He would drive the ball cross-court and there was no way you could get the shot. He was very mean and had no mercy when it came to tennis. I knew how hard it was for Dad when he finally had to give up tennis due to advanced Parkinson's. Actually I could follow the course of his dreaded disease by the way Dad played tennis.

I can remember how hard it was for Dad to come home after a difficult week away at work because my mother, by Friday night, was distraught and had had it. For five days she had been a single parent for five children, three of whom were in diapers. My father would try hard on the weekends to give Mother a break. By Monday morning, when he went back to work, it would be a lot calmer.

As a mother of two teenagers, I can't imagine what it would be like taking care of five kids for five days without the help of your husband. Our friend Elaine Foreman used to call my father the "feminist" of that generation. Dad would change the diapers, clean the house and fix the meals. Women who were friendly with my parents were very jealous of Mom and wished their husbands would be as helpful. My father tried to share equally when he came home. I felt that he helped raise us, which was pretty tough considering all the responsibilities he had at work.

Dad would walk into this scene after an exhausting week traveling back and forth building Comcast, one of the most successful businesses in the United States, and we never knew about it. We had no idea what my dad was building. He was not flamboyant about his success in business. He was the opposite, a brilliant and intellectual man who was modest and tried hard to please his wife when he was home. We always knew how much he loved Mom. He adores her. It was a difficult time but he helped supply us with a secure and loving home life.

If we asked Dad what he did at work he would draw us a picture of two mountains with lines drawn between the two.

"This is what I am doing. I am providing TV for people who live in-between these two mountains by putting up a cable." That was all we knew. I remember talking with my best friend. Her father was making a middle-class salary of $2,000 a month. To me, that sounded like so much money. I came home and told Dad what I had just heard:

"You can't believe what my friend's father makes." In retrospect I am sure he must have been making twenty times that amount, but he would never let us know.

There was a discount store called Artie's on Wadsworth Avenue where we shopped for our clothes and where Mom would also buy her clothes. One day I overheard the following conversation:

"Gerrie, you don't have to shop at Artie's any more." That was the first time my mother realized Dad's business was going well. I think that is when I realized that we were no longer part of the lower working class.

It wasn't until I was in my teens and out of the house that I realized that my dad was building an empire. I read about it in the paper. My friends knew about it and they were the ones who bought it to my attention.

Through my teen-age years I was very rebellious and closed myself off from the rest of the family. I was a liberal thinker interested in all the protests of the day. I was part of the anti-war movement, trying to discover who I was. I was pretty preoccupied with that in the late 1960s. During that time I made it very difficult for my parents. But my father was always there waiting for me at the door. No matter what time of the night it was, if I was out late and hadn't told them where I was going, he was always there. I used to tell him, "You really don't have to do this," but way down deep, I liked that my father was there for me. He was paying attention to what I was doing. He stayed right with me during that whole rebellious time. He hung in there, and I appreciate that. This experience brought us together, but our real closeness developed later in life. As he became ill, we developed a more open relationship.

My father, because of the suicide of his parents and the succession of foster homes, always had a stiff upper lip and "just kept going." He couldn't allow himself to recognize his own feelings. I feel that he has done that all his life. He never let us know about the Holocaust, and he never talked about his parents. He just tucked it all away.

It was only after he became sick that he slowed down. As he started losing the abilities that he had, Dad started to open up to reveal things about himself that he never wanted to think about before. Writing his memoirs has given him an opportunity to finally revisit his past. He always had to keep going just to survive. The Parkinson's made him stop and reflect, but he didn't feel sorry for himself.

He has made his illness an opportunity to grow, and that's the lesson we can all learn. You can make anything into a positive experience, and that's what I think he is doing. I have adopted it as my model; just keep on going. Have a stiff upper lip but keep on going.

Jimmy, a building contractor in Texas:

My dad wasn't around a lot because he traveled a great deal. Even when he was in the Philadelphia area, we would see little of him during the week. He would come home late at night, have dinner, then he and Mom would talk about the day's events.

Weekends were different: An activity that my father and

I did regularly was to play tennis. Wall Park was close to our home and sported tennis courts. Interested players would gather for pick-up games. Dad and I would warm the bench until there were enough players for a foursome. I was a good player as a little kid, and Dad seemed proud of the way I played. He must have thought I was pretty good, for I was the only kid there. Playing tennis with Dad as his doubles partner was something I looked forward to doing.

As I grew older and my tennis skills improved, Dad encouraged me to continue playing. There was a group of kids in our area who were good, and in order to encourage us, we were invited to play at an indoor court in Willow Grove. Play started in the wee hours of the morning before the court officially opened for business. I remember it being very dark when Dad would "dnock" me awake and drive me to practice.

Dad had a special way of waking us up in the morning. Walking around in his underwear (it seems he was always in his underwear), he would go from room to room making a deep aboriginal clicking sound by placing his tongue on the roof of his mouth and then releasing the sound. The noise sounded like, "dnock," "dnock," "dnock." Dad would cluck at our doors until he heard movement and then move on to the next. After dressing, we would arrive downstairs to find that Dad had made us the worst eggs imaginable. Soft-boiled and matzo eggs were his specialty. Mom was allowed to sleep in. There would be no "dnocking" in her ear.

While in high school I became involved with Dad's company, Comcast. I wanted to see what was outside the confines of Cheltenham High, and I wanted to earn some money. In the summer of 1970 Dad got me a job in Meridian, Mississippi, one of his original CATV systems, as an installer. I was fifteen at the time, not old enough to drive a car. I remember clearly getting my social security number and going down there and having my first real job.

The South then had a reputation of being very red-necked and conservative and very racist. My thinking was to the left, liberal. I must have sounded like a chip off the old block. As an installer, I would ride around on the company truck and attach the cable from the street to the home, known in the trade as a "drop." We were given a schedule in the morning and would go from "drop" to "drop" throughout the day. The homes in which I worked were in the poor black areas of town. I had the illustrious duty of going under the house to make the last connection that would take the cable through the floorboards into the home. It quickly became evident that this neighborhood did not have any sewers or cesspools since all the contents of the toilet ended up on the ground beneath the house. Making my life even more miserable were the hostile roosters that I had to keep at bay. I learned quickly the difference between the haves and the have-nots and what it was to be poor and black in the South in 1970.

My dad was very good at working with the local politicians because his sincerity came through. It was this success in getting franchises from the large towns that helped build Comcast.

Before leaving on Monday morning for his trip to Mississippi or elsewhere, he would say to us, "Take care of your mother and listen to her. Don't give her a hard time or she is going to have a nervous breakdown." Of course that went in one ear and out the other.

Weekends Dad would jam us in the station wagon, pile the bicycles on the car rack, and drive to Fairmount Park where we would all enjoy a bike ride along the Schuylkill River.

Dad drove a Beetle, which surprised me because it was a German car. Dad's rationale? It wasn't the same government, and he held no grudge. He had no anger or hostility towards the people who now owned VW.

Being athletic, I never stopped playing some kind of game in or out of the house. Many times after dinner, the living room would be filled with prone bodies of my brothers and me wrestling on the floor. It did make Dad more than a little nuts.

Dick Fosbury was a champion high-jumper of the day who had a unique style. He jumped with his rear end or backside first, rather than the conventional way of front first. It sounds screwy but he won a lot of meets with this technique. Kenny and I decided that we would emulate Dick. Pushing the beds together in our bedroom, we would hook one end of a blanket into the doorjamb and close the door so the blanket would stay taut. With the aid of one of us holding the free end of the blanket to regulate the blanket's height, the other would attempt the "Fosbury Flop." We were very serious about perfecting our skills. There was only one problem; the higher we raised the blanket and the greater height we achieved, the more noise it made when we hit the beds. Admittedly, the whole house would shake. My father, who would be reading in the living room, would come running up the stairs as fast as he could. By the time he entered our room, the beds were back in place and the blanket had vanished. Dad would be beside himself with fury. After admonishing us severely, he would return to the lower floors only to have the scene repeated. Now that I am forty-five and have kids of my own, I have no idea why he didn't kill the two of us.

I was in my early teens when Dad was elected chairman

of the N.C.T.A. On one occasion he was good enough to take me to one of his weekend meetings. As head of the national association, he was treated like royalty. I remember we were driven around in limousines from place to place all weekend. There was a party at every event and they were very lavish. For one event, they rented the whole museum of art and each room had a different table of food.

In the summers our whole family, all seven of us, spent a lot of time down at Long Beach Island. The Pauls, Sheldon and Ruth, were special friends and neighbors, and at the end of the summer we used to put on a talent show. As kids we had a great time preparing our skits to perform in front of the assembled group. One year after our performance there was a knock at the door. We had not noticed that Dad had slipped out of the room during the show. There was my dad at the door with a funny hat on, wearing a wig of long hair, with a cigarette dangling from his mouth, clothed in a Nehru shirt and bell-bottom pants.

One of the most outrageous porn movies of our day was *Deep Throat*, starring Linda Lovelace. Of course, unknown to our parents, we went to see it at the local theater. I entered the theater with my brother Kenny and some friends and we took our seats, hoping the lights would go out before anyone noticed our presence. The lights dimmed and the movie started, much to my relief. Unfortunately, halfway through the showing, the film broke and the manager turned on the lights. There, sitting on an aisle seat, was none other than my father.

Dad's admission:

"I timed my entrance into the theater with the beginning of the movie to make sure I wouldn't be seen by any of my kids or their friends. I had planned to exit just before the end of the movie for the same reason. You can imagine my surprise and chagrin as the lights came up."

When bikinis were the rage, there was an elderly fellow who would arrive at the Barnegat Light beach in his scant swimsuit; we named him Bikini Bob because he looked so ridiculous. One day while we kids were enjoying the beach, Dad, not to be upstaged by anyone, arrived beachside in a loincloth hooked to a scant strap. We all took cover; we certainly didn't want to be associated with him.

Kenny, who is employed in the financial department of Comcast:

Our family always had a place at the New Jersey shore, mainly at Barnegat Light, where we would spend free weekends and the summers. Dad loved to teach while we were in the car going somewhere, especially on the two-hour trip to and from the shore. Latin seemed to be a favorite subject and he would question us on the Latin roots of English words. Out of self-defense, I took Latin in the seventh grade. He would quiz us all the time when we were in the car, so this was not always a relaxing time. It was fun for him because he felt that everyone was as intellectually oriented as he, but not everyone is.

While at the shore my father tinkered around the house. He would never go to the beach, although once a year he would make a ceremonial trip to the ocean and take a swim. He was a sailor, and his favorite activity was being on the bay in his sailboat.

Our sailboat was moored a short distance from shore at the Twenty-fifth Street beach. The depth of the water at the mooring was hip high. Dad hated to get his pants wet.

To the constant embarrassment of his children, he would remove his pants and, holding them high in the air, would proceed to the anchored boat in his underwear.

I have an excellent ear for music. I can pick out and play on the guitar both the tune and chords of most songs, and can improvise in the various scales. My father, however, once took harmonica lessons for two years and for his last lesson was still practicing the songs from his first lesson. He never learned to play a single song without a mistake (let alone well enough for another person to discern the song). Enough said about his musical ability!

Dad's and Mother's tardiness is legendary. They are invariably late to everything. At my wedding they arrived an hour late, blaming it on a stuck elevator in their apartment building. At a friend's wedding, we were so late that our family missed the entire ceremony. To their embarrassment, as they went through the reception line praising the beauty of the service, I piped up, "But we missed the ceremony."

One fall we were going to services at Rodeph Shalom for the High Holy Days and, because of my parents' tardiness, we had to sit on folding chairs in the back of the auditorium. Dad had briefed us on the service and explained that the high point in the service was the blowing of the ram's horn, known as the Shofar. We were to listen very carefully, for the Shofar did not have a mouthpiece, was very difficult to play, and at times nary a sound could be produced by the Shofar-blower. Adding to our interest was the knowledge that one of Dad's good friends was the Shofar-blower.

The service dragged on and we *rutched* in our seats waiting for the triumphal moment. When it came, we found that we couldn't see Dad's friend so we climbed up on the seats to get a better look. As the blasts of the *"Te-keeah Gedolah"* reverberated in the synagogue, the folding chairs collapsed, dumping us kids on the floor and making a terrible racket. It certainly was a new way to start the new year.

Jud, an assistant U.S. attorney in Philadelphia's Department of Justice:

Dinner was a time when the whole family sat together. Dad's Bible was the *New York Times*. He liked to pick editorials in the *Times* and read them at dinner. He liked the idea of indoctrinating us into liberal Democratic politics. He would then use these readings as a springboard for discussion. We would spend a lot of time talking about politics or one of the latest books. I grew up thinking that was the norm. It was not until much later in life that I found that wasn't so. Most families sit around talking about other family members or what their day was like. Not in our family.

My father was very neat and orderly. Perhaps that was the German in him, but things had to be picked up and put in place. I am not neat, and maybe that was my rebellion. We had endless fights because my socks were lying in the middle of the floor, or because I had dumped my dirty shirt on the floor, or because I was not cleaning up my room. These were daily occurrences, and it was always about how sloppy I was. When I went to a friend's house in the neighborhood I would invariably get a call:

"Jud, your father is on the phone."

I'd go to the phone and hear, "Jud, you get back here and clean up your room."

Dad just couldn't stand anything out of order.

My father had a wonderful tradition when it came to celebrating birthdays. On our birthdays, Dad would take each of us out for breakfast to the restaurant of our choice. Although the choice was ours, in order to please my father and knowing where he wanted to go for breakfast, I would always pick Linton's, Dad's old Temple hangout.

We used to make day trips to the Pine Beach Yacht Club, and when we went out to dinner it was never easy to order with five young kids. Upon sitting down at the table, my father would pick up the menu and then announce, in a loud voice, the price ceiling:

"OK, you can order anything up to $3.75 on the menu."

The waitress would come over and my dad, thinking he would expedite matters by standing up, would read the items off the menu:

"OK, now who wants the spaghetti, who want the lasagna, who wants the . . ."

In 1963, Mom and Dad came down to the New Jersey shore looking for a summer house. They bought land on the bay side between Twenty-sixth and Twenty-seventh streets in Barnegat Light. In 1967 they build a house large enough to house seven Aarons. In the late 1980s they knocked the old house down, and builder Michael Spark built the present one in its place. Buying the original land was my mother's idea. My father was convinced that the whole island was going to wash away. Every time Father drove across the causeway onto Long Beach Island he was convinced the island was going to sink and that it was going to be his car that sunk it.

My father was terrified of storms. There was some rational basis to his thinking because Long Beach Island, during one of the infrequent hurricanes, had been cut in two in the 1960s. Nonetheless, he was unduly concerned about storms and being washed away. I remember one night there was a thunderstorm accompanied by lightning and serious rain, but not a true hurricane. He woke us up in the middle of the night and told us we were abandoning ship, we were getting off the island. He piled the family in the car and drove off the island in the middle of the storm, which was probably far more dangerous than staying in our summer home. We stayed on the mainland in a local motel. Waking the next day I looked out the window to see a calm, sunny day with a cow standing outside my window. Nothing could have looked more peaceful. We slinked back onto the island, and I am sure he had to take quite a ribbing from all of his neighbors and friends.

Although sports were not my thing, playing the saxophone was. I became quite proficient and spent ten years playing professionally. I even had the thrill of playing with B.B. King and others of his caliber. In the mid-eighties, when I was a professional musician, I was interviewing for a job as the high school jazz band director at Haverford High School. I went into my interview with the superintendent and the principal of the high school. Halfway through the interview the principal, who had said nothing up to this point, leaned across the table and, looking at my resume, said,

"Aaron, Aaron, any relation to Dan Aaron?"

"Yeah, he is my father."

The principal continued, "I am Mel Drucken and your father had the biggest single influence on my life. He is the reason I am doing what I am doing today."

I thought to myself, "This job is in the bag," and it was. As it turned out, Dad had been Mel's counselor at S.G.F. They had not seen each other for years, but following my employment they renewed old ties.

I am sure that what happened to Dad in his childhood

had an effect on him as a father, on his value system, and on how he wanted to bring us up. A colleague of Dad's came up to me at Dad's retirement and said, "Your father was really the social conscience of Comcast and the cable industry."

Dad brought this compassionate facet of his personality to business as well as to his family.

Thirty years ago Dad, along with Ed Espen, Val Udell, Leonard Cooper and a group of other interested parties, started a camp for economically deprived kids, which they call Woodrock. They rented for a dollar a year a ten-acre plot of land from Fellowship Farm near Pottstown. It was really a human-relations project. My parents sent me there for three years and now I am on the board of directors.

Alison, who is a public defender for the state of New Jersey:

I was the youngest and I reaped many of the benefits because my older siblings, who "broke in" my parents to some extent, paved much of the way for me. I had a lot of freedom. I was able to ride my bike around the neighborhood, go to friends' houses, or go into Jenkintown or Philadelphia when I wanted to because, thanks to my siblings' experience, my parents knew that it wasn't the end of the world if I was away for a few hours.

On the weekends, when Dad was home, my earliest and most pleasant memories are of my father and me listening to music together. He would sit in his den and smoke his pipe or, infrequently, cigars. I used to scream at him that cigars were too smelly. He would put on show tunes and sometimes opera and I would dance and sing. For that moment in time I was "Daddy's little girl," and I loved that feeling. There are pictures of me dancing to *The Sound of Music,* and Dad wrote the inscription "Daddy's little girl" in one of the photo albums.

The Ogontz Junior High School track wasn't far from our house. Dad would put on his generic blue sweat suit (he was too tight to buy a nice sweat suit) and on his ears he would stick these big fat headphones with big antennae sticking up out of it, making him look like an air-traffic controller. And that's the way he would go to the track and run. I would go with him, riding my bike. He set an example of how to keep in shape, for I too am now a runner.

I was fortunate enough to go to some of the N.C.T.A. conventions with Dad when he was chairman of the organization. It was kind of neat to see famous people in the field of cable coming up to my father and talking with him. It was then that I realized that my father was an important person. I loved the schmoozing that went on and the HBO guys who gave away pens and jackets. I thought that was just like Hollywood.

In the hospitality suite, I wanted to meet someone famous, so I went up to Ted Turner. I was a pretty precocious teenager for a sixteen-year-old kid, and I said something like, "You have a sailboat. I have a sailboat."

I said that to engage him in conversation. He completely blew me off and I was devastated. I guess I should have told him that I was Dan Aaron's daughter.

When he was home, Dad and I played a lot of tennis together, but he would always use these dinky little drop shots to get his points. I wanted him to slam the ball at me, but for whatever reason, he wouldn't do that, and it was those "dinky little drop shots" that got me.

I spent a lot of time on Long Beach Island with my parents. I was always amazed by the kind of social life they had; they were out every night. My dad had a terrible time remembering people's names. As they dressed for the occasion, the scenario would always be the same. Dad would ask,

"Now where are we going tonight and what's the name of our host and hostess? Who else is going to be there and what are their names?"

My father was the one who taught me how to sail. I loved to sail and became quite proficient. We used to sail up to the Dutchman's Restaurant on the causeway that connected Long Beach Island with the mainland. I was able to sail right up to the dock even though it was a difficult maneuver, for the wind was invariably blowing right at us. My parents used to put me on display to anyone who would look. They would get a kick out of showing off their daughter who could stop on a dime.

Depending on the direction of the wind, Dad and I would sail down to the Dutchman's or across the bay to Captain's Inn. Mom would follow in the car with shoes and with anyone else who wanted to go out for lunch. Sometimes we would go to the Dutchman's on a whim and find that we in the boat only had two pairs of shoes with us. That meant two of us went into the restaurant and held a table. Then one would return to the boat with the shoes so the others could come into the restaurant. Many times I found myself in Jud's shoes, which of course were much too big.

Dad knew just how to embarrass us. When we would go to Captain's Inn we would request "she-crab soup," a family favorite. Before the waitress filled the order Dad would stand up at the table and, in a loud voice, would ask:

"How do you tell a he-crab from a she-crab?"

Reluctantly, we would all say, "I don't know Dad, how?"

"Throw it against the wall, and if it says, 'Ouch my balls,' it isn't a she-crab."

Dad's "thing" was that he liked to ask questions. When people came over to the house, whether it was a friend from school or, God forbid, a guy that I might be interested in dating, Dad would start with his twenty-question routine. After being questioned, my boyfriends never wanted to come back. They thought they were being interrogated. What they did not realize was that my father was genuinely interested in people and this was his way of learning more about them.

Dad would also interrogate "the gas guy" who pumped gas into the car. We were always embarrassed, because by the time we got $15.00 worth of gas, Dad knew where the gas attendant was from, how much schooling he had, what his parents did and how much he made pumping gas.

Dad was a dour kind of guy; he wasn't like other men who would laugh and smile. He sort of had a "puss on him" most of the time. This visage made people think he wasn't approachable, when actually he was one of the most approachable people around.

One day, in the late 1970s, I noticed Dad had President Jimmy Carter's picture on his bathroom mirror.

"What's that for?" I asked.

"Well, I know I don't smile very much and now that I am chairman of the N.C.T.A., I have to learn how to smile. President Carter is trying to help me."

When Dad disciplined you, you were scared. He made you feel really bad about whatever it was that you had done. The worst sin you could commit was making Mother do more work or hurting her feelings. He was so protective of her. If we did something wrong and she said, "Oh, now you have done it. Wait until your father gets home," that was the worst. Looking back, I think that was great. He really protected Mom's authority.

Dad never used to hug us. He wasn't much for hugs. In fact, when he did hug us it was a very wooden kind of hug. I couldn't take that kind of treatment, and I decided I wasn't going to let him get away with it. So, I started making him hug me. When he would hug, I would stay there in his arms and hug back.

We learned from our parents, especially Dad, the need to give back to our community. Jud, Erika and I are all in public-service careers, and the Geraldine and Dan Aaron Family Foundation allows each of us to support the causes in which we are interested.

Love you Dad, and you did learn how to hug!

At Barnegat Light in the early 1960s — Erica, Jimmy, Kenny, Jud, and Alison.

To conclude these recollections, I asked my longtime friend, David A. Long, to add his own thoughts about our collaboration in writing these memoirs.

David A. Long, retired CEO of the LLB Group:

It was Dan's eldest daughter, Erika, who persuaded him to write his memoirs before his Parkinson's disease progressed any further. Dan and I started this project in September of 1999.

As Dan put it, "David arrived in my living room at the shore with his laptop and said, 'OK, Dan, let's write your memoirs.'"

Our beginnings were difficult. By his own admission, Dan was nearly "dead in the water." Almost completely non-ambulatory from his nineteen-year bout with Parkinson's disease, and wearing two hearing aids, he spoke quietly of times long past. It was difficult to hear what he was saying. His voice was slow, his thoughts labored. He spoke in broken sentences, the words stumbling from his mouth. As he searched the depths of his past, his eyes stared blankly into space; it was as though he was recalling a movie of long ago.

Amazingly, the process of writing his memoirs revived him. Within a month, his voice became stronger and my typing became faster.

As he rolled the imaginary movie and the recollection of a specific episode became difficult, tears would fill the corners of his eyes. When I reacted to his words with, "How ghastly" or "That must have been terrible for you," the tears dried and a wonderful smile lit his bearded face.

His whole karma changed by the time we had finished his recollections of the Holocaust. For whatever reason, Dan came out of his shell; he had a *raison d'être*. Once an avid swimmer, Dan had lost his ability to swim as the disease progressed, and would sink to the bottom of the pool like a stone. Curiously, as his memoirs unfolded, he found that he could swim again.

During the fall and early into the new year, we met three or four times a week to talk and record. I visited him at his home in Sarasota, Florida, in mid-January and reworked the first ten chapters. One day, when we broke for lunch, Dan decided to get out of his wheelchair and use his walker to go to lunch. I couldn't believe my eyes. I nicknamed him Rip—as in Van Winkle.

February and March found us separated by a thousand miles while I researched the beginnings of the cable industry and perused Comcast's annual reports and Dan's many speeches. Our separation also gave me the opportunity to interview the many family members, friends and colleagues who enjoyed reminiscing about their favorite subject, Dan Aaron.

Dan and I were back together again in late spring and then in the fall to finish. I was the receptor, the recorder and the analyst of information from the past. I listened, questioned, and then typed Dan's thoughts into my laptop, transposing the material into a coherent narrative.

The story of Dan Aaron's life is a story of one man's struggle under impossible circumstances. To be trusted to put onto paper the memoirs of such a courageous human being has been a highlight of my life.

Dan says, "David, I never could have done this without you."

I say, "What a rare privilege to have worked so closely with such a remarkable human being."

Notes

1. Michael Berwick, *The Third Reich* (New York: G. P. Putnam's, 1972), p. 32.

2. Jules Doneson, *Deeds of Love: A History of the Jewish Foster Home and Orphan Asylum of Philadelphia — America's First Jewish Orphanage* (New York: Vantage Press, 1996), p. 103.

3. Anna Kest Mantinband, *The Mills of the Gods* (privately published, 1978).

4. Anna Kest Mantinband, *A Time to Remember* (privately published, 1979).

5. *Counselor's Handbook,* Samuel G. Friedman Vacation Camp (Collegeville, Pa.: S.G.F. Vacation Camp, 1949).

6. Stephen E. Ambrose, *Citizen Soldiers: The U.S. Army from the Normandy Beaches to the Bulge to the Surrender of Germany, June 7, 1944–May 7, 1945* (New York: Simon & Schuster, 1997), p. 274.

7. Ibid.

8. David McCullough, *Truman* (New York: Simon & Schuster, 1992), p. 481.

9. *New York Times,* December 17, 1972.

10. Thomas P. Southwick, *Distant Signals* (Overland Park, Kans.: Primedia Intertec, 1998), p. 17.

11. *New York Times,* December 22, 1950.

12. Author's interview with Julian A. Brodsky, February 4, 2000.

13. George Plimpton, "Easier to Follow Football on Cable Television," *Summary Annual Report, 1974* (Philadelphia, Pa.: Comcast Corporation, 1974), p. 8.

14. Author's interview with Tom Wheeler, September 6, 2000.

15. *New York Times,* November 10, 1981.

16. *Summary Annual Report, 1999* (Philadelphia, Pa.: Comcast Corporation, 1999), p. 4.

Acknowledgments

My sincere thanks to my friends, who gave unstintingly of their time for hours of interviews: Ralph J. Roberts, Chairman, Comcast Corporation; Julian Brodsky, Vice Chairman, Comcast Corporation; Abe Patlove, Vice President, Comcast Cable Division; Sam Buffone, retired Manager, Comcast Cable; Barbara Lukens, retired Vice President, Comcast Cable Franchise; Dave Watson, Director of Merchandising and Vice President, Comcast Cable Division; Morris Vogel, Acting Dean of Temple University Liberal Arts College; Tom Wheeler, Executive Director, Cellular Telecommunications Industry Association; Harold S. Goldman, President, Jewish Federation of Greater Philadelphia; Dr. Howard Hurtig, Executive Director, Movement Disorders Center at Pennsylvania Hospital in Philadelphia; and Jane Wright, M.S.S., Program Coordinator for the Movement Disorders Center.

Many people helped to make this book a reality: Thomas P. Southwick, who provided valuable source material; Jimmy Hirschfeld, retired Director/Producer of *Captain Kangaroo,* who culled through the manuscript as only a producer/director could; Rabbi Elliot Holin, who reviewed the manuscript with a scholarly eye; Peter Bauland, Professor of English, University of Michigan, who treated the manuscript like a term paper, correcting both the English and German; Marie Molchen, secretary extraordinaire; Susan Madison, Director, the Barco Library, The Cable Center, Denver, Colorado, who offered invaluable production suggestions; my longtime friend, Patricia Ann Long, who read and reread the manuscript, making helpful suggestions at each stage to improve the text; Adrianne Onderdonk Dudden, book designer, who transformed my 8½ x 11-inch manuscript into a 6 x 9 hardcover book; my editor, Nancy Steele, to whom I am indebted for her expert guidance; and Barbara York, Senior Vice President, Industry Affairs, National Cable Television Association, who helped to launch this book.

Most of all, my thanks to Gerrie Aaron, my understanding and feisty wife of more than fifty years.

Index

References to photographs are printed in boldface.